THE INDIAN PRINCES IN COUNCIL

Owing to the antiquity and rarity of this book, certain pages are regrettably absent, and readability is compromised due to the blurring of the original text. If you possess any insights regarding the availability of these missing sections, kindly inform us. Your assistance is crucial in ensuring the completion of this significant work for the benefit of future generations.

THE INDIAN PRINCES IN COUNCIL

A RECORD OF THE CHANCELLORSHIP
OF HIS HIGHNESS
THE MAHARAJA OF PATIALA
1926-1931 AND 1933-1936

BY

K. M. PANIKKAR

GYAN

Published by

Gyan Publishing House
5, Ansari Road
Daryaganj, New Delhi-110002
Phone: 011-47034999, 9811692060
E-mail: books@gyanbooks.com

Distribution Network
gyanbooks.com
India, USA, Canada, UK, Australia

ISBN: 978-81-212-8460-8 (HB)
First Published, 1936

2nd Impression 2024

Printed at: Gyan Press, Delhi.

THE INDIAN PRINCES IN COUNCIL
Author: K. M. PANIKKAR

THE INDIAN PRINCES IN COUNCIL

THE INDIAN PRINCES IN COUNCIL

A RECORD OF THE CHANCELLORSHIP
OF HIS HIGHNESS
THE MAHARAJA OF PATIALA
1926–1931 *and* 1933–1936

BY

K. M. PANIKKAR
Author of
Indian States and the Government of India
The Portuguese in Malabar
Federal India (jointly with
Colonel Sir Kailas Haksar)

WITH A FOREWORD BY

LT.-GENERAL HIS HIGHNESS
THE MAHARAJA OF BIKANER
G.C.S.I., G.C.I.E., G.C.V.O.

OXFORD UNIVERSITY PRESS
LONDON : HUMPHREY MILFORD
1936

FOREWORD

THE question of the position of Indian Princes in the polity of India and the Empire has to-day especial interest in view of the Constitutional Reforms. Mr. Panikkar's narrative of His Highness the Maharaja of Patiala's Chancellorship of the Chamber of Princes, therefore, appears at an opportune moment.

To some extent it may be said that the form in which that question was raised, and the federal proposals themselves, are the outcome of the activities of the Chamber of Princes, which—at least since 1922, when I was its Chancellor—had pressed for a careful examination and inquiry into the future position of the Indian States.

The Chamber of Princes was instituted, as Mr. Panikkar points out, as the result of the desire of the rulers of Indian States for an organization which would enable the Viceroy and the Princes to come together and to deliberate on matters relating to the Empire, India, and the States as a whole. That great and far-sighted Viceroy, Lord Hardinge, who found informal consultation with Princes valuable during the critical days of the Great War, was sympathetic towards this idea. The Princes' Conference came into existence in 1916 and continued to meet every year till the Chamber of Princes was formally inaugurated in 1921.

As Honorary General Secretary to the Princes' Conference from 1916 to 1921, and as the first Chancellor of the Chamber of Princes from 1921 to 1926, it fell to my lot to shoulder the responsibility of organizing and conducting, on behalf of the Princes and States, the work of the Conference and the Chamber.

Throughout this period of ten years His Highness the Maharaja of Patiala was closely associated with me as a valued colleague in much important duty, including that of working out a preliminary scheme while on a small Committee of Princes assisted by some Ministers, and, at a later stage, the formulation, in collaboration with the officers of the Government of India, of the final proposals relating to the establishment of the Chamber, its constitution, rules, and regulations, its functions and composition, and other allied matters; and on various important Conferences and Committees, and especially the present Princes' Standing Committee.

When, in 1926, I decided to relinquish the Chancellorship, it was my privilege to propose at an informal meeting of the Princes the name of His Highness the Maharaja of Patiala as my successor; and he subsequently bore the burden and responsibilities of that difficult, and at times unenviable, office for a total period of some eight and a half years.

Notwithstanding occasional differences of opinion—trivial or important—which are inevitable in public affairs, I am happy to feel that our official relations to-day are marked by the most cordial co-operation and consultations, and that the friendship which began some thirty-four years ago has been further strengthened and cemented.

I also had the pleasure of enjoying the personal friendship of the Maharaja of Patiala's revered father; and His present Highness has for a great many years extended to me the privilege of an elder brother.

I am thus in a position to speak from considerable first-hand knowledge of His Highness the Maharaja of Patiala's great work—both inside and outside the Chamber of Princes—and of his personal contribution to the problems which faced the Princes during one of the most important junctures in the modern history of the Indian States.

It is, therefore, with great pleasure that I write this Foreword.

On questions such as those dealt with in this book there is bound to be divergence of views; and it should not be considered that I subscribe to all that Mr. Panikkar has written in graphically describing the work with which he has, in no inconsiderable degree, been associated. Those who read *The Indian Princes in Council* will find that it is a useful contribution to the political history of the India of recent times.

GANGA SINGH,
Maharaja of Bikaner

BIKANER,
August 1936.

CONTENTS

APPENDIXES

CHAPTER I

INTRODUCTION

A BRIEF introduction setting forth the conditions and circumstances immediately preceding the Chancellorship of the Maharaja of Patiala is perhaps necessary as an historical background for a correct appreciation of the work done by His Highness as Chancellor of the Chamber of Princes.

The Conferences of 1913 and 1914, convened by Lord Hardinge to ascertain the views of the Ruling Princes on special subjects touching their Order, were the first and tentative attempts towards a collective organization of Princes. The experience gained and the benefits which resulted from these meetings gave rise to a general desire that such conferences should be held annually. Lord Hardinge, who, like his predecessor Lord Minto, appreciated the value of the co-operation of Princes in matters of all-India or Imperial concern and was fully alive to the strength that the British Government would derive from the collective support of the Princes, naturally welcomed the suggestion of an annual gathering of Princes. A Conference of Ruling Princes for the discussion of general questions affecting the States and British India was summoned by him annually in conformity with this wise policy, which was followed also by his successor, Lord Chelmsford. H.H. the Maharajadhiraj of Patiala was associated with these annual conferences from their inception. He took a prominent part in the discussions and was from the beginning an accepted leader of opinion in the princely circles. When Mr. Montagu came out to India in 1918, the Maharaja, who had already achieved an outstanding position among the Princes, was, along with His Highness of Bikaner and the late Maharaja Scindia, prominently associated with all the important discussions of the time. In fact, it was at His Highness's invitation and at Patiala itself that the momentous meeting of Princes and Ministers in 1918 took place, at which the views of the Princes with regard to constitutional reforms and their claims in regard to their States were first formulated.

At this meeting, besides Their Highnesses of Bikaner, Alwar, and Patiala and Ministers like Sir M. Visvesvarayya, Col. (now Sir) Kailas Haksar, and Sir Manubhai Mehta, there were also present British-Indian statesmen of the repute of Lord Sinha, the Rt. Hon. Sir Tej Bahadur Sapru, the Rt. Hon. Srinivasa Sastri, Pandit Madan Mohan Malviya, and Sir Ali Imam. The question of the relations of the States with the Government of India was thoroughly discussed, and the drafts prepared at the earlier meetings held at Bikaner and Alwar were further revised. The final views of the Princes emerging from these discussions were embodied in a memorandum, and the Conference also drew up a draft scheme for establishing improved relations between the Government and the Indian States. This scheme was informally handed over to the Government of India during the discussions on constitutional reform.

In April 1918 the Montagu–Chelmsford Report on the Indian Constitutional Reforms was published. Chapter X of the Report, which dealt with proposals relating to Indian States, was discussed by the Princes at their Conference in January 1919, when various Sub-Committees were appointed to examine the recommendations of the Report. H.H. the Maharaja of Patiala was a member of all the important Sub-Committees and his work in this connexion was much appreciated by his brother Princes. As an outcome of these deliberations a comprehensive scheme was embodied in a series of resolutions recommending the creation of a permanent Council of Princes, the appointment of a Standing Committee, the acceptance of the principle of Commissions of Inquiry (and a defined procedure in connexion therewith), and the establishment of direct relations between the Government of India and the important States in the Provinces. These resolutions were forwarded by the Government of India, along with their own recommendations, to the Secretary-of-State in May 1919. The decisions arrived at by the Government were communicated to the Conference by the Viceroy in November 1919, when the Princes were informed of the intention of the Government to call into being a permanent Chamber of Princes, and they were invited to undertake the task of formulating their proposals in that behalf. They were also informed of the decision of the Government of India and His

Majesty's Government to adopt their proposals regarding the appointment of a Standing Committee.

The Chamber was formally inaugurated in February 1921 by H.R.H. the Duke of Connaught on behalf of His Imperial Majesty. From the time of its establishment the Maharaja of Patiala was a member of the Standing Committee of the Chamber and was elected to that body every year. Besides serving on the Standing Committee His Highness also worked on the Committees relating to riparian rights and to the question of the honours, dignities, and ceremonials of the Princes. Besides, on the different Ministers' Committees which prepared the material for the Princes, a representative of His Highness's Government was always given a place. In 1924 the Maharaja was nominated as the Officiating Chancellor of the Chamber of Princes in place of H.H. the Maharaja of Bikaner, when the latter went to Geneva to attend the League of Nations Assembly as a member of the Indian Delegation.

A detailed account of the work done by the Chamber from 1921 to 1926 is not germane to this narrative. But here it may be stated that besides its ordinary routine work the Chamber during this period was occupied mostly with the task of perfecting its constitution. Many of the questions left over from the Codification Committee were also taken up, and where final resolutions were not reached much spade-work was done enabling the States to understand their exact position in regard to many of the vital administrative problems, where political practice had grown up in a manner detrimental to their interests.

The Chamber, though active in these directions, was more interested in the vital question of the States' future position. The actual experience of the working of the recommendations contained in the Joint Report, which were in a measure the counterpart of the liberalization of government in British India, proved unsatisfactory in many directions. An instance in point is the recommendation in regard to the Court of Arbitration. This had been duly accepted by the Government of India by their resolution in the Foreign and Political Department No. 427-R dated the 29th of October 1920, but it was, as the Butler Committee put it, 'unfortunately never acted upon'. The working of the Montagu–Chelmsford Act also aroused apprehensions, as in the economic and fiscal sphere the Government of India came practically to be dominated by British-Indian interests, and even in the political sphere the Paramount Power became apparently less able to give protection to the States against movements directed against them from British India.

From the very beginning the Indian Legislature began to press for a widening of the Act and for a further measure of reforms. The Princes, while not desiring to stand in the way of British-Indian reforms, desired to safeguard their own position. Though this was the predominant motive in their mind and they made no secret of their opinion that this was the one question that they desired to be discussed, the machinery of the Chamber afforded no opportunity for its consideration. Realizing the vital importance of this question in 1922, the Maharaja of Bikaner, then Chancellor, put forward a proposal for an informal Round Table Conference of the Princes with the Viceroy and his advisers; and again in 1924, after consulting his colleagues, he approached H.E. the Viceroy with a definite request for the appointment of a committee to inquire into this question. But Lord Reading considered that no useful purpose would be served either by a Round Table Conference or by a committee, and in spite of persistent efforts it was not possible to achieve anything in this connexion. It was at this juncture that the Maharaja of Patiala was elected Chancellor of the Chamber of Princes, and we shall see in the next chapter what steps he took and what results he obtained on this most important question.

It may perhaps be useful at this stage to mention briefly in the following pages the arrangement that was adopted. The Maharaja of Patiala's actual Chancellorship extended to over eight years, without counting the periods during which he only officiated. For the purpose of this narrative the period has not been taken up year by year but treated as a whole. The Maharaja of Patiala held the office from 1926 to 1936 with an interval of two years during which the late Maharaja Jam Sahib of Nawanagar and H.H.

the Nawab of Bhopal were each Chancellor for a year. Thus the Patiala Chancellorship falls into well-defined periods: 1926 to 1931 and 1933 to 1936.

This procedure has been adopted to trace in an uninterrupted manner the development of the various activities of the Chamber. These activities have been varied and have covered a wide range of subjects. In their present treatment they have been classified under the following broad headings:

(1) Maintenance of the rights and the privileges of the Princes.

(2) Codification and simplification of the political practice.

(3) The recognition and appreciation of the position and rights of the smaller States.

(4) Indian States and the problem of British-Indian reforms.

(5) Improvement of the working of the Constitution of the Chamber.

(6) Safeguarding the States under Federation.

Some important documents of an historical character have also been added as appendixes.

CHAPTER II

DETERMINATION OF THE RIGHTS OF THE STATES

THE main work to which the Maharaja addressed himself on being elected Chancellor in 1926 was the determination of the rights of the States in the political and economic sphere. It had long been felt by the Princes that the vague and inchoate character of their relationship with the Paramount Power was fraught with serious danger to their future, especially in view of the possibility, which was becoming increasingly clear, of a general transfer of political power from British into Indian hands. The Montagu–Chelmsford Reforms which had been inaugurated five years earlier were having results on the States which were neither anticipated nor desired by them. On matters of common interest to British India and the States, the Indian Legislative Assembly, representing British India exclusively, was exercising an authority which, at least in the economic sphere, completely ignored the interests of the States. The change from free trade to protection, which the Indian Legislature initiated, affected detrimentally the fiscal and financial interests of the States for the benefit of British India. The indirect taxation, which the reformed Government increasingly embarked upon, affected the peoples of the States and crippled the financial resources of their Governments. Politically, also, the Legislature began to claim coextensive powers with the Government, thus pretending to an authority over the Indian States which was justified neither by the facts of history nor by the theory of law. Speaking before the East India Association on 23 July 1928 in regard to this practice, His Highness said:

'I need not go into details, which, indeed, are being authoritatively investigated in another place, but I will simply say that one glance at the map of India, from the standpoint which I took at the beginning of my address, might have convinced those who were legislating for British India in 1919 that anything which they did for those portions of India not under the rule of the Princes must necessarily affect, both directly and indirectly, the portions over which the Princes held sway. In a great variety of directions, for example, the fixing of the rupee ratio, the introduction of protective duties, experiments with prohibition, and the like, we have found ourselves most deeply and vitally affected by policies in the framing of which we had no hand. Even before 1919, as I have already hinted, we had imagined that something of the kind might happen; and it was for this reason that we laid such stress upon the Chamber of Princes, as providing an institution upon which might be based some machinery for joint consultation between the Indian States and British India, in matters of common concern to both. But I must confess that the actual working of the Reformed Constitution in British India, and the degree to which our interests were affected without our knowledge or control, came as a surprise to all of us. Hence it was that our previous desire to obtain the machinery of which I have spoken became strengthened into a request for an authoritative examination of the whole of our position.'

Again, writing in a British review, the Maharaja said:

'I would only ask my readers to consider what happened in 1919. A Reformed Constitution was set up in British India. Did any one in England ask how the rights of the States would be affected? No; and the result is that the popularly elected legislatures in British India to-day are taxing the States, without their consent, in a variety of directions; are penalizing them heavily in the spheres of tariffs, excise rates, salt, opium, and the like, for the benefit of the British-Indian Exchequer and for the greater prosperity of British India.'

The constitutional writings of the time, especially of such eminent British-Indian leaders as Sir Sivaswamy Aiyar, would show that they were looking forward to the day when the British-Indian Central Government would inherit from the Crown the full armoury of paramountcy and would be able to exercise its prerogative powers in the same way as does the Cabinet in England—a position totally inacceptable to the Princes and the States. As the Chancellor said in a statement on a later occasion: 'We and our people will never submit to being governed by British India, over many parts of which our States in former times held sway.' At another time His Highness said:

'In fact, they [British-Indian leaders] seem to assume that British India would absorb or at least have full authority over the Indian States. Such an idea, we of the States, peoples and Rulers alike, are bound to oppose with all our strength.'

This position was fully appreciated by the Viceroy, Lord Irwin, who, in his opening speech in the Chamber of Princes in November 1926, said:

'It is becoming every day more clear that the future relations of the States with the Government of India are matters of the greatest moment, and I am anxious that this question should be examined with the greatest possible care from every point of view. I do not suggest that any action is immediately necessary. But frank discussion can do nothing but good, and I therefore propose, for the consideration of Your Highnesses, *that the Chamber should authorize the Standing Committee to hold informal talks with me and my advisers, whenever I think this might most advantageously be done.* I lay emphasis on the fact that such conversations would be entirely informal. They would pledge none of those taking part in them to any conclusions. Their object would be simply to clear our minds on a subject of great complexity and great importance, and I know that they would be useful both to the States and the Government of India. I, therefore, ask Your Highnesses to consider my proposal with care and sympathy.'

Accordingly the following resolution was moved by the Maharaja of Patiala and passed by the Chamber:

'That the Chamber do authorize its Standing

Committee, with the addition of such Princes and expert advisers as may seem desirable, to confer with H.E. the Viceroy and his advisers, as suggested by His Excellency in his address to the Chamber at the opening of the present session.'

It will be observed that the suggestion contained in the above statement of H.E. the Viceroy not only gained for the Princes that for which they had been bargaining for a very long time, but it also marked the beginning of a process of change in the very character of the functions of the Chancellor and the Standing Committee. As a result of this change the Chancellor and the Standing Committee came to be recognized as the representatives of the Princely Order. By achieving the position of an intermediary between the Viceroy and the Chamber, as the only recognized and accredited body competent to carry on negotiations with the Viceroy on behalf of the Chamber of Princes, the legitimate functions and responsibilities of the Chancellor and the Standing Committee were for the first time defined and established. What the Chamber was able to achieve in the years that followed, especially at the Round Table Conference, was due almost entirely to the recognition of this constitutional position.

Immediately after the conclusion of the session of the Chamber of Princes His Highness set about the work of collecting the necessary material for the Conference with the Viceroy. Circular letters were issued making confidential inquiries and requesting information on matters likely to be raised at the Conference. A Conference of the Rulers and Ministers was convened at Patiala in February 1927, to which certain leading British-Indian statesmen, including Lord Sinha and Sir Tej Bahadur Sapru, were also invited. The results of deliberations of the earlier meetings held at Bikaner were placed before this Conference with a view to evolving, if possible, a definite scheme for the consideration of the Indian Princes as a body. The Conference recommended that the Standing Committee should request the Viceroy to appoint an independent committee for the purpose of investigating the many points which touch the position and the interests of the Princes in general. An *aide-mémoire*[1] was prepared, giving in brief outline the considered view of the Princes on vital constitutional questions, and as this document forms what may be termed the groundwork of all later negotiations, it will repay detailed and careful study. It may be said to summarize the policy which the Maharaja of Patiala followed with unwavering fidelity.

The Maharaja recognized from the beginning that the consolidation of the external position of the States was dependent, to a large extent, on the creation of modern administrations and the maintenance of good government within the States. The question of internal reforms was always one of difficulty, and was rendered especially so by the demand in British India for democratic government within the States. Besides, the Indian States being in different states of evolution, it was impossible to lay down a scheme of reforms suitable to all. States with more or less advanced democratic governments like Mysore, Travancore, Cochin, and Baroda, with well-established modern administrations like Hyderabad, Gwalior, Kashmir, Jodhpur,

[1] Quoted as Appendix I.

Bikaner, and Patiala, could not be classed in this matter with States where the administrations continued to be medieval and the Ruler looked upon his State as a private domain for his enjoyment. The Chancellor, however, felt that the time had come when the question had to be frankly faced. After consultation with his advisers, and with the approval of the Viceroy, Lord Irwin, he evolved a scheme which may be called 'the minimum of good government applicable to all States'. The scheme was circulated to the Princes by the Chancellor in a letter dated 25 February 1927. In it the Chancellor impressed upon his brother Princes the desirability of effecting the following reforms in State administrations where they did not already exist:

'(1) A defined Privy Purse not exceeding 10 per cent. of the total revenues of the State; thus setting free the rest of the revenues for the improvement of the administrative machinery, the development of our States, and the amelioration, from every point of view, of the moral and material condition of our subjects.

'(2) A competent and independent Judicial Committee which will exercise by delegation the powers inherent in the Ruler of a State in regard to judicial and other matters, reserving for our own consideration the exercise of the royal prerogative of clemency.

'(3) A solemn declaration that the servants of the State would be removed from office only for proved misconduct after full and fair inquiry.

'(4) The association with ourselves of Ministers in some kind of a Cabinet which will secure continuity of administration.

'(5) The maintenance of a police force which shall be effective instruments for the preservation of the rule of law. This implies that a State Police should consist of men of good character, adequately paid, and officered by superiors trained in the knowledge of their duties.

'(6) The adoption, by specific enactment in each State, of codes of law, which should consist of the laws in force in British India, with such additions and alterations as local circumstances may require. The supersession of law by executive order should be rendered impossible; and in order to afford scope for material development by means of the creation of industries and the attraction of capital, comprehensive commercial laws should be enacted on modern lines. Upon this step a claim should be based for the

> amendment of the law of British India in such a fashion as to recognize the procedure of the States' Codes as procedure under the laws of British India.'

As a result of the Conference the Viceroy, Lord Irwin, was persuaded to recognize the necessity of having the nature of the relationship between the States and British India properly examined and defined. This was, indeed, a truly notable achievement. The relationship between the States and the Crown, which extended now for over a century and a quarter, had remained nebulous and inchoate. That the Rulers were sovereigns in their own States, and that the Crown had obligations, duties, and responsibilities to them by virtue of their treaties and engagements, was recognized. But the nature of that relationship and of that complex of duties, obligations, and responsibilities, known as paramountcy, had never been examined or defined. For the first time the necessity for such an examination was recognized. As the question was new and its nature complicated, it was necessary to subject it to a preliminary examination by constitutional lawyers of repute, and with this object the Chancellor sent Colonel (now Sir Kailas) Haksar and Mr. Rushbrook Williams to England with instructions to consult the most eminent counsel available and to obtain from them an authoritative opinion on the existing position. The lawyers consulted were the Rt. Hon. Sir Leslie Scott, K.C., M.P. (now Lord Justice Scott), Mr. Wilfred Greene, K.C. (now Lord Justice Greene), and Mr. (now Sir) Donald Somerville. The opinion which these distinguished lawyers gave only strengthened the desire of the Princes to have their case thoroughly investigated. His Majesty's Government also agreed with the suggestions of the Viceroy that the problem should be examined carefully, and for that purpose appointed the Indian States Committee with Sir Harcourt Butler as Chairman.

The appointment of this Committee, which consisted of Sir Harcourt Butler, Colonel the Hon. Sydney Peel—an economist and financier with international experience, and Prof. (now Sir Ernest) Holdsworth, a jurist of eminence, with Colonel (now Sir George) Ogilvie as Secretary, threw on the Chancellor's shoulders new and greater responsibilities. The case for the States, varied and bewildering in its complexity and often conflicting, had to be prepared. Materials, such as they were, lay buried in the archives of States whose guardians preserved them with jealousy from the eyes of all outsiders. A hundred years of political somnolence had, in the case of many States, led to an ignorance, inconceivable to-day, of the rights of the States, and where such rights were cherished the documents were often incomplete. Besides, the time at the disposal of the Chancellor was short. The Maharaja, however, faced the situation calmly; and, with the support of the Standing Committee, decided immediately to appoint a senior Minister closely connected with the work of the Chamber from its inception and with wide experience and profound knowledge of Indian States affairs—Colonel K. N. Haksar—to undertake the preparation of the case for the States. No selection could have been more appropriate, and under his guidance the work of collecting, arranging, and preparing the material for presentation to the Butler Committee was taken in hand without delay.

The presentation of the case required distinguished lawyers, and for this purpose His Highness, at the suggestion of his brother Princes, engaged Sir Leslie Scott, who was invited to come out to India and study the situation on the spot.

All this organization and activity involved very heavy expenditure. It was necessary to collect a special fund for this purpose, and the Chancellor himself set an example to his brother Princes by starting it with a magnificent donation of Rs. 5 lakhs. This lead was followed by other Princes like Their Highnesses of Kashmir, Bhopal, and Bikaner.

As was but natural in a case which affected the Princes of India as a whole, many difficulties were experienced before the work could be undertaken. It was only the trust and confidence that the Chancellor's personality inspired among the Princes, and his own unshakable determination, that made it possible for the Special Organization for preparing the material to continue with their labours. A large number of States were hesitating to place their case in the hands of the Special Organization. The smaller

States were loud in their complaint that the Special Organization was unlikely to attach importance to their cases. Local rivalries and jealousies also contributed their share to the difficulties. These difficulties, which would have daunted a less courageous man, only made the Maharaja more determined. First of all he secured an assurance from the Viceroy that, so far as His Excellency and his Government were concerned, the States need have no fear in supplying the Special Organization with the necessary material. Even this assurance having been found insufficient, His Highness convened special meetings of Princes at Patiala and at Bombay, where the necessity of presenting collectively the case of the States was explained to the Rulers.

In order to secure the support of the smaller States, the Chancellor held a conference of the Rulers and representatives of such States, and every attempt was made to dispel their misgivings and enlist their support. Practical unanimity having thus been secured, it became possible for the Maharaja of Patiala to put up a strenuous fight in the interests of the States as a whole.

When the Committee sat in England to hear

the evidence, His Highness, as Chancellor, deemed it desirable to be on the spot, at great personal inconvenience and expense, in order to direct the presentation of the case of the States. The public activities of the Maharaja in the interests of his Order during this visit to Europe extended over a wide range. He spoke at public gatherings, like the Royal Institute of International Affairs and the East India Association, where his speech was broadcast, and even before the Committee[1] itself. The comprehensive manner in which the case of the States was presented and the insistence with which it was urged by His Highness and, under his instructions, by Colonel Haksar and Sir Leslie Scott are well known. The four volumes covering over 6,000 printed pages of foolscap paper in which the material supplied by the States was analysed, edited, summarized, and arranged, constitute a standing monument to the work done at the time. If the claims of the States are better known and more widely appreciated to-day, if the States themselves are aware of their rights, dignities, and authority, if the

[1] Appendix II.

procedure in regard to many matters is being rectified, the credit in no small degree belongs to the Maharaja of Patiala, who, as Chancellor, was in supreme charge of all the work connected with the States' side of the case.

The Butler Committee published their Report in February 1929. Though it accepted the claims of the States that their treaties were with the Crown, and that the relationship thus established could not be transferred to a new Government without their consent—a point of no small importance—and also held that, whether or not a State makes a contribution to the cost of defence, the Paramount Power is under a duty to protect it, the Report, unfortunately, did not afford satisfaction to the Princes on the main question of paramountcy. The Committee's dicta, such as 'Paramountcy must remain paramount', 'it must fulfil its obligations by defining and adapting itself to the necessities of the time and the progressive developments of the States', and 'usage lights up the dark places of the treaties', seemed to leave the States in a worse position than before.

This situation, naturally, created considerable

dissatisfaction among the Princes. Even before the Report was published a resolution had been moved and passed in the Chamber of Princes that the Government of India should take no action on the recommendations of the Committee until the opinion of all the States, the Rulers of which are members of the Chamber in their own right, had been received and the Report, together with the opinions of the States, fully discussed in the Chamber. The same resolution requested H.E. the Viceroy to give an opportunity to some of the Rulers, whom His Excellency might select, to explain to him verbally their views on the Report.

Accordingly, as soon as the Report was published, His Highness obtained His Excellency's consent for the Standing Committee to confer with him at Poona on the 28th of June 1929, before the departure of the Viceroy on leave for England. It was known that Lord Irwin was visiting England with the object of discussing with H.M. Government the question of summoning the Round Table Conference for talking over the question of constitutional reforms. It was considered imperative that the views of the Princes should also be before the British Cabinet when the question of Indian Reforms was being discussed. For this purpose it was necessary that the views of as many Princes as possible should be ascertained, and a representative opinion formulated on the issues dealt with in the Butler Report. The Chancellor, therefore, convened an informal meeting of the Princes at Bombay on the 24th of June 1929, and issued the following timely warning:

'Your Highness will appreciate that no final opinions on the report can, and should, be formulated by any State unless the Princes have had an informal discussion among themselves, and have tabulated a representative resolution embodying the consensus of opinion on the report. Accordingly, I would suggest that at this stage Your Highness may send a preliminary expression of opinion, which may be reconsidered in the light of the decisions reached at the Bombay informal meeting, and the opinions then finally adopted may be forwarded to the Government of India, so that the various important points involved in the report may be fully considered, individually and jointly, by the various States before they finally commit themselves to any definite views.'

A series of important resolutions was passed

at the Conference held at Bombay, and these were handed over by the Standing Committee to the Viceroy when they met him at Poona.

In August 1929 His Highness circulated these resolutions to all the members and representative members of the Chamber, and also a brief statement of his own views on the various paragraphs of the Report of the Indian States Committee.

At the session of the Chamber of Princes (February 1930) the Report was fully discussed and the following resolutions were adopted:

'(1) Resolved that

(*a*) this Chamber is of opinion that the grant of a Sanad by the Paramount Power confirming to a State a right which inherently belonged to it does not entitle the Paramount Power to claim that it has created that right in the exercise of its paramountcy;

(*b*) that this Chamber is of opinion that no Sanads imposed by the Paramount Power can supersede previously existing treaties or engagements between it and a State.

'(2) Resolved that this Chamber is of opinion that the time has arrived to revise its constitution and to enlarge its powers.

'(3) Resolved that this Narendra Mandal is of opinion that matters affecting the personal and dynastic status of Rulers should be the subject of decision by H.E. the Viceroy, as representative of the Crown, in consultation with selected members of the Order of Princes.

'(4) Resolved that this Chamber recommends that suitable machineries should be available as of right to adjudicate upon all matters of justiciable nature and to arbitrate finally upon those of non-justiciable nature in issue between the British Government or British India and the Indian States or between the Indian States, *inter se*, provided that in the last named case both parties agree to the employment of these machineries. In case they do not, the present method for settlement would continue.

'(5) Resolved that this Chamber requests H.E. the Viceroy to appoint an independent expert body to explore the fiscal claims of the States after ensuring that the personnel and terms of reference are settled in agreement with the Standing Committee of this Chamber.

'(6) Resolved that this Chamber considers that the time is now opportune for defining by joint consultation between the nominees of H.E. the Viceroy and those of this Chamber the bases of intervention in the internal affairs of the States.

'(7) Resolved that this Chamber is of opinion that the doctrine of Usage and Political Practice as expounded by the Indian States Committee is neither sound in its conception nor fair in its application to the relations subsisting between the Crown and the Indian States. That doctrine has in the past been the cause of serious and unjustifiable encroachments upon the internal sovereignty and autonomy of the Indian States which are recognized by solemn Treaties, Engagements, and Sanads.

That a course of practice followed with respect to individual States by the Political Department of the Government of India in certain eventualities which has neither been consistent nor uniform, or to which from time to time exception has been taken by the States concerned, or which arose during minority, joint administration, or any such interregnum when the Government of India held the position of trustee with respect to the State concerned, cannot afford any basis for intervention by the Government of India to the prejudice of the acknowledged rights of the States.

'(8) Resolved that this Narendra Mandal places on record its considered opinion that the true relationship of the States with the Crown is founded upon—

(*a*) treaties and engagements which bind parties and

(*b*) usage which is established by mutual consent.

This Narendra Mandal is therefore of the opinion that the obligations of the Crown and the States arising under the two aforesaid heads remain unaffected by the doctrine of Paramountcy referred to in the Indian States Committee Report.

'(9) Resolved that this Chamber recommends the creation of effective machinery for the settlement by mutual agreement of matters of common concern to British India and the States.'

These efforts were not in vain, for even before the meetings of the Chamber of Princes in February 1930, H.E. the Viceroy had made his historic announcement of 31 October 1929 regarding the Indian Round Table Conference, which was received with great satisfaction by the Princes. In respect to the recommendations of the Butler Committee the Viceroy also declared, in his opening address to the Chamber of Princes, that a minute and detailed consideration of them must await the report of the Simon Commission.

It will thus be seen that the first five-year period of His Highness's activity as Chancellor has had the following results on the constitutional position of the States:

(1) It established the position, never accepted

before by the Government and contested by British India, that the treaty relationship of the States were with the Crown;

(2) that the relationship could not be transferred without the consent of the States to a new Government in British India;

(3) that the States were by their treaty entitled to be defended free.

The acceptance of these propositions secured for the States a powerful voice in determining the future of India and in assuring the safety of their States in the political changes of the future. The remarkable change in their constitutional position, which was evidenced by the influence which the representatives of the States exerted at the Round Table Conference and the discussions that followed, was in no small measure due to the Chancellorship of the Maharaja of Patiala. In fact, from being silent and impotent partners His Highness converted the States of India into active and powerful principals in the policy of India.

CHAPTER III

ROUTINE WORK OF THE CHAMBER

IN January 1919 the Conference of Princes appointed a Committee to examine the proposal for the simplification, codification, and standardization of political practice. The Committee was supplied with a list of twenty-three questions which the Government of India had prepared from the references received by them in response to the inquiries made from the States on the subject of the encroachment of political practice on their dignities and prerogatives. Later on, when the Chamber of Princes was inaugurated, the Codification Committee was replaced by the Standing Committee of the Chamber of Princes and the examination of the twenty-three points was entrusted to it.

At the time when H.H. the Maharaja of Patiala became Chancellor of the Chamber of Princes, the following subjects out of the list of twenty-three points had already been disposed of by the Chamber:

1. Telegraphs and telephones in the Indian States.

2. Construction of railways in Indian States.
3. Wireless telegraphy and telephony.
4. Compensation for railway land in Indian States.
5. Acquisition of residential property in British India by Ruling Princes.

Besides, other matters brought up before the Chamber had also been finally disposed of, namely:

1. Mining concessions in Indian States.
2. Assessment of compensation for land required by the railways in Indian States.
3. Courts of Arbitration: suggested amplification of Foreign and Political Department Resolution thereon.

Owing to various causes, to which it is unnecessary to refer here, many of the questions included within the twenty-three points could not be taken up in the early years of the Chamber. It is not surprising, therefore, that after his election as Chancellor of the Chamber in January 1926, His Highness found himself confronted with a long list of pending subjects, and it is mainly due to His Highness's businesslike treatment of these subjects that most of them had either been finally disposed of or had reached a stage of considerable progress before the expiry in 1931 of the first five years' period of His Highness's Chancellorship. A list of the subjects which came up for discussion before the Standing Committee of the Chamber during this period is given below:

1. Questions relating to the honour, dignity, and ceremonials of Princes.
2. Matters relating to the reorganization of the Indian States Forces and other allied subjects.
3. Radio broadcasting in British India and its application to Indian States.
4. Restrictions imposed on the possession, purchase, and importation of arms and ammunition for the personal use of Rulers of the States.
5. Representation of the States on the Railway Board, the Rates Advisory Board, and the Tariff Board.
6. Construction of dams in Indian States.
7. Revision of the Rules for the Administration of Indian Peoples' Famine Trust.
8. Provision of a school at Satara for junior officers of the Indian States Forces.
9. Air navigation in Indian States.
10. Dealings between Indian States and capitalists and financial agents.
11. Powers to be given to Councils of Administration

of Indian States to offer troops to Government in emergency in the absence of the Ruler from the State.

12. The privilege of exercising censorship over telegrams.
13. Acquisition of non-residential property in British India by Ruling Princes and Chiefs.
14. Settlement of boundary disputes between Indian States.
15. Jurisdiction over railway lands.
16. Application of the principle regarding assessment of compensation, arrived at in respect of tramways, to cases for compensation when road railways are constructed.
17. Codification of international law.
18. Marking of weights on heavy packages transported by vessels.
19. International conventions on the treatment of foreigners.
20. The protocol on Arbitration Clauses and the Convention on the execution of foreign arbitral awards.
21. Seating arrangements at investitures.
22. Education and training of minor Princes.
23. Road development.
24. Relief to subjects of Indian States for the payment of double income-tax.

25. Mints and coinage in Indian States.
26. Construction of tramways in Indian States.
27. Extension of the Fugitive Offenders Act, 1881, to Indian States and administered areas.
28. Division of reparation payments due from Germany between British India and the Indian States.
29. Procedure for consulting the Standing Committee and the Chamber before resolutions are passed.
30. Question of amending section 45 of the Code of Civil Procedure 1908 (V of 1908) to enable Civil and Revenue Courts in British India to send their decrees for execution to the Courts of Indian States.
31. Question of giving publicity to the proceedings of the Chamber of Princes.
32. Question of linking inter-State telephones.
33. Employment of Europeans, &c., in Indian States.
34. Assessment of compensation for land required in British India and in Indian States for irrigation purposes, &c.
35. Reciprocity between British India and Indian States as regards the recognition of previous conviction awarded by Courts of States or of British India.

36. Contribution made by the Indian States and other Rulers towards charities and other public causes of benefit to India, in times both of peace and of war.
37. Leadership of the Indian Delegation to the League of Nations.

Out of the questions mentioned above, the following fourteen subjects were finally disposed of during the Maharaja's first period of Chancellorship.

1. Radio broadcasting in British India and its application to Indian States.
2. Air navigation in Indian States.
3. Dealings between Indian States and capitalists and financial agents.
4. Acquisition of non-residential property in British India by Ruling Princes and Chiefs.
5. Construction of tramways in Indian States.
6. Employment of Europeans in Indian States.
7. Assessment of compensation for land required in British India and in Indian States for irrigation purposes, &c.

Agreement was also reached on the following fourteen questions:

1. Provision of a school at Satara for junior officers of the Indian States Forces.

2. Powers to be given to Councils of Administration of Indian States to offer troops to Government in emergency in the absence of the Ruler from the State.
3. International conventions on the treatment of foreigners.
4. The Protocol on Arbitration Clauses and the Convention on the execution of foreign arbitral awards.
5. Seating arrangements at investitures.
6. Road development.
7. Relief to subjects of Indian States for the payment of double income-tax.
8. Reciprocity between British India and Indian States as regards the recognition of previous conviction awarded by Courts of States or of British India.
9. Leadership of the Indian Delegation to the League of Nations.
10. Mints and coinage in Indian States.
11. Procedure for consulting the Standing Committee and the Chamber before resolutions are passed.
12. Question of amending Section 45 of the Code of Civil Procedure 1908 (V of 1908) to enable Civil and Revenue Courts in British India to send their decrees for execution to the Courts of Indian States.

13. Question of giving publicity to the proceedings of the Chamber of Princes.
14. Question of linking inter-State telephones.

Considerable progress in the way of exploration and preparatory work was made in regard to other subjects.

When dealing with the routine work of the Standing Committee and the Chamber during this period it is necessary to state that most of His Highness's time and attention were occupied in the formulation and direction of the policy of the Chamber in relation to the more important questions of Constitutional Reform in British India and the position of the Indian States in the future government of the country, and consequently the work of the simplification of political practice had, of necessity, to suffer. Nevertheless, the agreement reached on various complicated questions shows that, in spite of obstacles, the Maharaja, during his tenure of office, did not overlook the importance of these subjects but devoted much attention to their satisfactory settlement.

The following extracts from the speeches of the Viceroy and of important Princes in the

Chamber regarding His Highness's work speak for themselves:

In November 1926 H.E. the Viceroy said:

'Your Highnesses will, I know, wish to acknowledge the ungrudging and conscientious manner in which H.H. the Maharaja of Patiala has performed the responsible duties of Chancellor during the past ten months. I have myself had ample opportunity of observing with what care he attends to the Chamber's work and interests.'

H.H. the Maharaja of Bikaner, moving a resolution of thanks to H.H. the Maharaja of Patiala in November 1926, observed:

'I have during the past ten years had so many reports to present, and so many occasions on which to inflict my speeches upon you—not to mention the large demand upon your time which I had to make yesterday in my very pleasant task when moving a Resolution of Welcome to His Excellency—that it is my desire to speak as little as possible on this and other occasions during the session.

'But I feel sure that I shall not be taxing the patience of the House when I state that we have listened with interest to H.H. the Maharaja of Patiala's survey of the work done by the Standing Committee during the past twelve months, and when

I perform the very agreeable task of moving a vote of thanks to H.H. the Chancellor. His Highness's statement to-day speaks for itself; and yesterday H.E. the Viceroy was pleased to bestow generous encomiums on the manner in which His Highness had performed his responsible duties as Chancellor during the past ten months.'

Again in 1928 His Excellency said:

'Your Highnesses will doubtless wish to express your appreciation of the energy and efficiency that have marked the tenure of his high and responsible office by H.H. the Maharaja of Patiala. He has been a watchful custodian of your interests while displaying promptness and courtesy in the conduct of business with my Secretariat.'

H.H. the Maharaja of Kashmir in 1928, in moving a vote of thanks to the Chancellor, said:

'Your Excellency, Your Highnesses, I rise to move a vote of thanks to my distinguished brother, His Highness of Patiala, who has so ably conducted the affairs of the Chamber and the Standing Committee for the past 15 months. I do not think it necessary to say very much about the work he has done. Your Excellency yesterday in your speech referred to the solid nature of the work that was performed by H.H. the Chancellor, and in the review that has just been presented to the Chamber, a detailed reference has been made to all that has been done.'

His Highness of Bikaner, in seconding the resolution, remarked:

'It affords me the most sincere pleasure in heartily supporting the vote of thanks to my brother and successor in the Chancellorship, H.H. the Maharaja of Patiala. His Highness's work as Chancellor has been by no means easy or light, and there could be no more fitting or greater testimony to the valuable services rendered by His Highness than the high tribute paid to him by Your Excellency in your inaugural speech yesterday. His Highness is carrying on the duties of Chancellor at a particularly important juncture in the history of our States, and should, as we hope, our expectations be realized from the recommendations of the Butler Committee and from what follows after that—we hope during Your Excellency's Viceroyalty—our Order will have still further cause to be grateful to His Highness of Patiala.'

The efficient discharge of the office of Chancellor by the Maharaja of Patiala was appreciated in the following terms by H.H. the Nawab of Bhopal:

'I should like to associate myself very heartily with

the vote of thanks which it is proposed to address to our Chancellor, His Highness of Patiala. I think we are all fortunate that the very important office of the Chancellor has been held by him for the last two years. I am sure those of Your Highnesses who have exercised the right to which we are entitled, of acquainting yourselves at first hand with the work which has been done, would have come to the conclusion that the Chancellor's office is efficiently run; that our letters and telegrams are promptly attended to; and that a great deal of very useful work is conducted entirely on the initiative of H.H. the Chancellor. Those of us who, like myself, are members of the Standing Committee, will have been very conscious during the last two years of the amount of time, care, and trouble which His Highness the Chancellor devotes to the common cause. The amount of correspondence that he has to dispose of in connexion with this work is something voluminous, and the readiness with which he responds to any call on his purse, time, and attention, clearly shows his self-sacrifice and devotion to the good of our Order.

'Further, it is not as if H.H. the Chancellor had had nothing else to do but to attend to our business. He is the ruler, and an active and energetic ruler, of an important State which possesses a highly organized administrative system. Nevertheless, he has found the time and energy to do all this work on our joint behalf.'

Regarding the volume of the work, His Highness of Bhopal said:

'In addition to these positive achievements you cannot, I think, be unmindful of the fact that during the period when His Highness of Patiala has been our Chancellor he has very sensibly and with great ability advanced the common cause. He has not only succeeded in increasing the attendance of the Chamber, but he has also accomplished the task, not at all times a very easy one, I fear, of enabling those of us who take a keen interest in the Chamber work to labour together in harmony, to pursue our common interests.

'Now I hope Your Highnesses will allow me to say that the record which I have briefly surveyed is no ordinary one. The success with which His Highness of Patiala has occupied the office of Chancellor is definitely proved: first, by the sheer amount of work which he has transacted, secondly by its striking results. These considerations are sufficient to make us truly grateful to him for the work which he has been doing on our behalf.

'I feel sure Your Highnesses will agree with me when I say that it has been a real asset to the whole Order of Princes that the office of Chancellor has been held at this particular moment by a Prince whose name has become proverbial for his open-hearted hospitality, for his extraordinary charm of manner, and for his most generous and open-hearted expenditure of his own resources in the common cause.'

In 1929 H.H. the Jam Sahib, speaking of the work of the Chancellor, said:

'Those of us who have worked with H.H. the Maharaja of Patiala can testify to the courage, the wisdom, the determination and the unselfishness which have characterized his services to our Order. During the difficult times of the last year, we have never found him wanting, and the clarity and vigour of his public pronouncements have been of the utmost service to us.'

His Highness of Dewas (Senior), in 1930, seconding the vote of thanks to H.H. the Maharaja of Patiala, said:

'I think it is only fair to state, and I trust H.H. the Chancellor will not object to the phrase, that he has been a very willing and a very loyal servant of the Order. I think it will be agreed that serving others is one of the greatest privileges of life, and while one who has willingly and faithfully served others is entitled to the rare satisfaction which can be derived from the consciousness of duty honestly performed, those who have been served owe to him the duty of publicly acknowledging their gratitude for such service.

'As I view the position, I can honestly say that we owe him much. We owe him the gift of the services for a protracted period of one of his ablest officers who has rendered valuable service. We owe it to him to acknowledge that throughout the past twelve months he has kept the wheels of the machinery known as the Chancellor's Secretariat moving. His very generous support has made it possible (of course with others of our large-hearted brothers) to achieve the work that has been done during the last eighteen months and more. Indeed, so keen is he in keeping us all up to the mark and so zealous in our cause that sometimes we have felt aggrieved at the flood of circular letters which continually pours down upon us with the noble object of ensuring that no matter of importance to our interests should be overlooked or their disposal delayed.

'In conclusion I would merely say that he has laboured incessantly in the discharge of his sacred trust and therefore he is entitled to our profound gratitude.'

Of His Highness's capability to conduct work during the sessions of the Chamber and his arrangement of business, the following extract from the Viceroy's speech is very eloquent and no further comment is needed:

'The general character of our proceedings seems to have been very businesslike and expeditious, and it is remarkable, I think, that we should have been able to conclude our programme of business within time, having regard to the immensely wide subjects that Your Highnesses brought forward for treatment on successive days.'

Nothing could be more indicative of the appreciation of the work of the Chamber under the Chancellorship of the Maharaja of Patiala than the decision of His Exalted Highness the Nizam in 1930 to contribute generously to the funds of the Chamber and its Special Organization. Referring to this fact in his closing speech in February 1930, His Excellency observed:

'There is one other matter which I should like to allude to before I sit down, that is the personal gratification—and I think in this matter I speak on behalf of all members of this Chamber—which I as its President have derived on learning of the decision of H.E.H. the Nizam of Hyderabad to associate himself with its work. I have little doubt that the Chamber is entitled to take that as a recognition of His Exalted Highness's judgement of the valuable work that the

Chamber is doing, and represents a desire on his part to strengthen the hands of those who are doing it. I find it difficult to exaggerate the importance to the general body of the States of the fact that His Exalted Highness would have thus publicly identified himself with the general organization of the States represented by this Chamber.'

CHAPTER IV

THE CHANCELLOR AND THE SMALLER STATES

THE Chancellorship of the Maharaja of Patiala marked an epoch in the relationship of the paramount power with the so-called smaller States. The term smaller States has been applied to the States whose Rulers have been excluded from the Chamber of Princes. Some of these States are larger in area and population than many enjoying higher salutes and greater prestige. For reasons which it is unnecessary to discuss here, their position was not fully appreciated in 1919–20, when the Chamber was being organized. Many of these States felt that a great injustice had been done to them, especially as the membership of the Chamber seemed to create a new differentiation. Naturally they looked upon the activities of the Chamber with suspicion and distrust.

When the Butler Committee was appointed and the Chancellor and the Standing Committee came to the conclusion that it was essential to put forward a united case, the position of these States and their attitude towards the work of the Chamber became extremely important. It was, however, no easy matter to bring them into line. Their suspicions were deep-rooted and not unnatural in view of the Constitution of the Chamber. The Maharaja realized their position and invited them to a special Conference to meet Sir Leslie Scott, who was then in India preparing the case of the States to be presented to the Butler Committee. In inviting the Rulers to this Conference the Chancellor issued the following circular letter:

'As you will have gathered from circulars which I have sent to you, I am hoping very much that you will find it possible to join with the Standing Committee of the Chamber in making a Joint Report for the betterment of our common interests. In this connection I think it is most desirable that you should have an opportunity of meeting personally the Right Hon. Sir Leslie Scott, K.C., M.P., who will present our case before the Butler Committee in England. If you would find it possible to come here on the 28th of March, or if any of your representatives would find it possible to come, I shall be only too happy to receive them. Sir Leslie Scott will be able to spend two or three days with me; and you will find it an excellent opportunity of telling him any of the principal points which you would like to be urged in the course of the representation to the Indian States Committee.

'Would you be so very kind as to send spare copies of this letter which I am providing, to your constituents?'

The foregoing circular letter was followed by one containing an invitation for another Conference of a general character at Bombay. At the latter Conference His Highness gave the following assurance to the smaller States:

'I want, in the first place, to say a few words as to the relations between the larger and the smaller States. From information which has come to me, I believe that the Rulers of the smaller States are in some instances hesitating to join with the Standing Committee because they fear that their own interests may suffer and that any change which is made in the present system will be of advantage only to the larger States and not to the smaller States. I believe that this hesitation arises from some misunderstanding as to what is the object of the whole scheme.

'I should like to ask the representatives of the smaller States one question. I know you are not satisfied with the present system. Would you not prefer a change such as we are also seeking, which will bring your affairs as well as ours, through the proposed State Council, under the influence of members of your own Order? We recognize the large interest which you, individually and collectively, possess; and we ask you to join with us in forwarding our common interest. If you will do so we will pledge ourselves to do our very best for you. The time is not ripe to speak of anything like specific guarantees, if only because we, like you, have still to vindicate our rights. But your interests and ours are common. Neither you nor we can improve the present position unless all the States, large and small, stand together.'

It was in this manner that His Highness was able to dispel the unfortunate misunderstandings which threatened to break the unity of the Princely Order. In fact, one of the important points to which His Highness directed his attention soon after his assumption of office was the position of the large groups of States in Bihar and Orissa, the Central Provinces, and the Simla Hills, whose powers were greatly restricted and whose authority was hampered in many ways. He had their cases thoroughly examined at the time of the Butler Committee, through the Special Organization which worked under his direct supervision. This examination convinced him that great injustice had been done in the past to many of those States and that it was his solemn duty as Chancellor to take up their case and rectify the position. In the evidence offered before the Butler Committee their case was specially stressed and the various disabilities under which their administrations were suffering were brought to light for the first time. Though it was felt by many at the time that the smaller States were being given undue prominence in the case presented before the Committee, the Chancellor, recognizing that the interests of all the States were equally concerned in removing the unjust restrictions on the powers of this class of States, stood his ground and insisted that the view taken by Counsel should be supported.

When it was found that the Report of the Butler Committee did not contain any recommendations in regard to the smaller States, His Highness directed that the matter should not be allowed to rest there and that the Special Organization should re-examine the whole problem and put it up for discussion in the Chamber and later with the Viceroy. In the public sessions of the Chamber in 1930, the question of the legal position of the States in Bihar and Orissa and the Central Provinces was raised on a resolution regarding the validity of Sanads. In the discussions with the Viceroy in July 1930 a separate Note on Sanads was submitted which attacked the position of the Government of India in regard to these States. That note, as it may be said to have changed the status of this class of Rulers, is quoted below in full:

'(1) In the practice of the Political Department the right claimed by the Government of India to issue Sanads has often been used to restrict the authority of the Rulers and to create new obligations. The two most conspicuous examples are the Sanads of adoption of 1862 and the Sanads issued from 1894 onwards to the Bihar and Orissa States.

'(2) The Sanads of 1862 were in fact intended to restore confidence and as such were only an assurance by the Government of India that the policy they had followed previous to the Mutiny of annexing certain classes of States on the failure of natural heirs will not be continued. The Government of the East India Company had claimed, on the basis of feudal theory, the right to refuse recognition in cases of adoption in certain classes of States. It is important to recognize that no such claim had been advanced as a universal principle. The claim was not to be made applicable to States which were in treaty alliance with the Company. As a result of the Mutiny the Government abandoned the position it had taken up and assured the States that the so-called doctrine of lapse would not be enforced. This is the true interpretation of the Sanads of 1862. It is clear that so far as the States in treaty alliance were concerned, the matter was never in doubt. Even in regard to others the Sanad was merely an acceptance by the Government that policy previously pursued was wrong and an assurance that no attempt would be made to resurrect that policy. It had, however, been argued that in issuing those Sanads even to States admitted to be outside the operation of the doctrine of lapse, the Government was conferring a boon, while it was actually only reassuring the States of its intentions and recognizing their inherent rights. In these Sanads the Government added conditions which have been adduced, among other arguments, to prove the acceptance by the Rulers of the reduction of their status *vis-à-vis* the Government of India.

'(3) It may be argued that it was open to the Princes to decline the Sanads of 1862, if they considered the condition attached to them unacceptable. In the first place, it might be emphasized that the Princes had only shortly before received Queen

Victoria's assurances in her proclamation of 1858, regarding respect of their rights and privileges "as her own". Thus these Sanads were in the nature of a "Surplusage". Secondly, the only condition laid down in the Sanad was that the Ruling family should be loyal to the Crown. The Princes could not therefore, even by a stretch of imagination, anticipate that the acceptance of these Sanads, which merely enjoined loyalty to the Crown, would be taken as an admission by them of their consent to the diminution of their status or the reduction of their sovereignty; for surely loyalty is the essence of alliance. That a diminution of status was deduced from the condition of loyalty in the Sanads would not be disputed. The Resolution of the Government of India on the Nabha case states that the acceptance of the Sanad of adoption gave them a right to intervene in the affairs of that State. The same argument was advanced in Lord Reading's letter to His Exalted Highness.

'(4) The Sanads issued to the Orissa States purported to define their status (already defined by the treaties and formal assurances of 1803 to 1829) and to confer on their Rulers titles, privileges and authority. These had been guaranteed to them by their treaties and formal assurances and were in no way derived from the British Government. And yet the Sanads of 1894 and subsequent years which by the wording of their preamble itself were meant only to define the relations in which these States stood to the Government of India, materially restricted their jurisdiction, imposed limitations on their executive authority, and attached conditions to their privileges.

'(5) It is clear that a Sanad by way of grant becomes a superfluity when the grantee already enjoys the powers which the Sanad purports to grant; when it proceeds further and restricts those powers its grant comes positively near to an act of usurpation. The Princes do not deny the right of the Crown to issue Sanads. When a Sanad grants either new rights or restores rights which had been ceded to the Crown, it may validly incorporate conditions and the grantee is at liberty to accept the Sanad or not, assuming that he is a free agent. If the benefits are accepted the conditions must also be accepted and such a grant becomes "a treaty by way of Sanad". But when a Sanad merely purports to define existing rights (as in the case of the Bihar and Orissa States), or is issued as an acknowledgement or admission of those rights by the Crown, it cannot create new obligations nor restrict rights which the other party is already enjoying.

'(6) But the practice of the Government of India has been based on the assumption that these Sanads can override treaties and engagements and render inoperative previous express limitations on the authority of the Crown. By the treaties of 1803 and 1829 the Orissa States were recognized to possess internal sovereignty including full rights of jurisdiction. Their hereditary titles and dignities were accepted and recognized. But by the Sanads of 1894 onwards not merely were these treaties overridden and the status of the Rulers reduced, but their authority and titles were declared to have been granted to them. Their jurisdiction was restricted and they were even forbidden to catch wild elephants in their own territories except by permission. Thus the Sanads seriously encroached upon the rights of these States which had been freely recognized before.

'(7) The view held by the Princes is that Sanads which have resulted from the necessity to acknowledge existing rights or to define existing status cannot impose new obligations or restrict the powers of the State. In other words, Sanads which do not confer any new right can only be considered as the Crown's formal acknowledgement of a right already possessed by the States. If the opposite point of view be accepted it will become within the competence of the Crown to reduce the powers and status of any State by issuing to it a Sanad and insisting upon its acceptance by the State and by a repetition of the process to abolish the State.'

The Government of India, it may be added, ordered an inquiry into the position of these States. The result is now well known. The Bihar and Orissa and Central Province States have been brought into direct relation with the Viceroy, and it is almost certain that those among them which are entitled to full powers will soon be admitted as members of the Chamber in their own right.

Again, ever since His Highness was first elected Chancellor he has striven untiringly to get the States which were in relation with the Provincial Governments into direct relationship with the Government of India. Almost in every speech which he, as Chancellor, delivered in reply to the Viceroy's address, this question was brought forward and its necessity emphasized. The following quotations from His Highness's speeches will prove the point beyond the possibility of doubt.

In November 1926 His Highness said:

'May we bring to the attention of your Excellency, and Your Excellency's Government, the strong desire, expressed by the majority of the Bombay States here represented, to be put on the same level, at an early date, as Western India States as regards direct political relations with the Government of India? Certain of the Simla Hill States have expressed a similar desire. In the case of the States of Rajputana, already in direct relations with the Government of India, the question of the simplification of these relations, and their conduct through a single intermediary, is one to which several of them have for long attached great importance. We are sure that in the case of such States as desire this simplification and have already expressed their desire, Your Excellency will yourself wish to afford them an opportunity of acquainting you with their point of view. At a time when, as we venture to think, the Indian States and the Government of India are arranging for close and adequate co-operation in the solution of problems of common interest, it is inevitable that the States not in direct political relation with the Government of India should experience a sense of disappointment, and an ardent desire for the increased dignity, and other corresponding advantages, attaching to such relations.'

In February 1929 His Highness said:

'In the next place we should like to invite Your Excellency's attention once more to the importance which we attach to bringing those States whose political relations are conducted by Provincial Governments, into direct relations with Your Excellency's Government, and to simplifying the relations through a single intermediary in the case of other States. We venture to hope that the complete execution of the policy enunciated in Chapter 10 of the Montagu-Chelmsford Report in this respect, will not be long delayed.'

In February 1930 His Highness said:

'As regards the question of bringing all the States into direct relations with the Viceroy, we have noted Your Excellency's remarks as to the difficulties of arriving at a decision in regard to this question at the present stage. Nevertheless, we beg to invite Your Excellency's attention to the principle enunciated in the Montagu–Chelmsford Report that on general grounds, relations between States and Government are clearly a matter for the Central Government, more especially as the growth of responsibility in the Provincial Governments cannot but unfit them in some degree to act in political matters as mere agents of the Government of India. We hope that the States which enjoy representation in the Chamber will at an early date receive the benefit of the change; what we ultimately desire is that all the States should receive the benefit of a common policy and be thereby spared differentiation which, as we know, has occurred, for example, in consequence of provincial rearrangements and which would, if continued, cause disappointment.'

In March 1931 His Highness said:

'Before we go on to the other points in Your Excellency's speech we desire once more to urge the early establishment of direct political relations with the States which are still in relationship with provincial governments. The importance which we attach to this question is known to Your Excellency as we have pressed for it year by year. The principle of this transfer was recommended by the Montagu–Chelmsford Report and recently by the Butler Committee. The administrative and political conveniences which will follow this change are indeed obvious. We may also be permitted once again to urge that the arrangements governing the present system of direct relations should be simplified so as to bring the States and their Rulers into closer contact with the Viceroy. We feel strongly that the time has arrived for these changes which we are convinced will result in administrative convenience and lead to better understanding.'

When the Round Table Conference was announced His Highness took particular care to see that a representative of the smaller States was also nominated. The Chief (now Raja) of

Sangli, who was nominated to represent that group, received the full and active support of His Highness, who reiterated on behalf of the Chamber the formal declaration of policy towards the smaller States already alluded to. The following extract from a letter addressed by the Chancellor to the Rulers of some of the smaller States would show the keen interest he took in securing equality of treatment for them.

'It is hardly necessary for me to say that the position of the Princes of the Standing Committee to-day is exactly what it was at the meeting held in Bombay in April 1928, and of course the whole of the States' Delegation, I am hoping, will speak in the name of the States of India.

'Your letter shows a certain amount of anxiety lest a distinction may be made between the larger and smaller States. You may take it from me that such distinction will not be emphasized by the Standing Committee whoever else might or might not suggest that a distinction should be made. Indeed, the fact that the Princes' Delegation includes His Highness of Sangli as specially the representative of the smaller States is, I hope, proof of the fact that the Standing Committee did not forget or overlook the interests of these States. His letter to you of the 18th June is merely in discharge of his special responsibility in the satisfactory fulfilment of which he will of course be assisted by the rest of us. And you will observe that that letter asks to know if there is "any special point of view" which the particular group of smaller States would desire to be specially put forward at the Conference. The idea behind the question apparently is that while the problem of the States as a whole would undoubtedly be brought forward in its broad aspects, no point of special importance to the smaller States should be overlooked. There is, I am sure, no idea that any distinction should be made, so far as the States are concerned, between the larger and the smaller States.'

Every care was taken to associate the smaller States with the deliberations in England, and on his return to India His Highness pressed for the nomination of the Rajas of Korea and Sarila to represent the non-saluted class of States in the Round Table Conference Delegation.

It was when the Maharaja felt that the activities of the Chamber were tending towards a neglect of the interests of the large group of States whose salute, area, population, &c., did not entitle them to be considered among the larger

States, that His Highness, relegating his own personal interests to the background and at considerable risk of being misunderstood, launched his now famous scheme of Confederation. His Highness fully realized that no scheme of Confederation, even if confined to the smaller States, would safeguard their interests against being neglected by the larger States and encroached upon by the Federation. At the meetings held at Bombay in 1931 this position was explained at length by His Highness, who assured the larger States that he was in no way against Federation provided that the large group of States, whose claims and interests were likely to be overlooked, were allowed to form themselves into a Confederation. When the larger States realized that His Highness's championship had united these States into a powerful body, they agreed to reconsider the whole question in the light of the confederal proposals. The negotiations which followed resulted in the Delhi Pact, which not only re-established the unity of the Princes, but also formulated in a specific manner the claims of the Princes in regard to the Federation.

His Highness's interest in the small States again led to his championing their claim for larger representation in the Federal Legislature. The Chancellor was from the beginning a supporter of a larger Upper House. In this, as in other matters affecting the welfare of the Princes, he had received the unstinted support of the Maharaja of Bikaner. It was through their united effort that the Upper House, which it was originally proposed should consist only of 60 members, became a House of 260. It was against a powerful combination of the larger States led by Sir Akbar Hydari and Sir Mirza Ismail, and supported by the Conservative leaders in England, that this victory was achieved. The Hyderabad and Mysore representatives held almost as a *sine qua non* that the Upper House should be as small as possible, not more than 80. The representation of the States in that case could not have been more than 32. The result would have been that a very large number of important States would have received only fractional representation in the Upper House and the smaller States would have been submerged in unwieldy groups. This proposal had the support of Sir Samuel Hoare and many other leading Conservatives and would certainly have been carried, with calamitous results to the States, if the Rulers of Patiala and Bikaner had not taken a firm stand at the time.

In a Note which His Highness, as Chancellor, wrote and a copy of which was sent to the Viceroy, the whole history of this important problem was traced and the views of the Chamber of Princes were stated for the information of H.M. Government. This note is quoted as Appendix III to this narrative.

It will thus be seen that to the very last the Chancellor fought, in every possible way, to secure for the smaller States fair and adequate representation in the Federal Legislature. It is no fault of either the Maharaja of Patiala or the Maharaja of Bikaner that the allocation of seats proposed by the Government gave effect to plural representation and that a large number of Princes who are members of the Chamber in their own right came to be given representation only in groups.

But it will be recognized at the same time that additional temporary weight has been secured for the States even if the entire body of Indian States do not join the Federation from the beginning. When the White Paper was published it was laid down that 'the intention is that a seat *allotted to an individual State will remain unfilled unless and* until that State has entered the Federation'.

Thus the claim which the Princes had put forward from the very first Round Table Conference was turned down in the White Paper. But the Chancellor, with the full support of the Standing Committee, considered it to be of vital importance that the influence and authority of the States should be preserved undiminished at any cost, and instructed the representatives of the Chamber at the Joint Parliamentary Committee to press this point and secure the full quota of seats, even if only the minimum number of States necessary to bring the Constitution into existence enter the Federation at the beginning. Substantially this has now been provided in the Act, and the credit for it must go to the Chancellor and the Standing Committee, but for whose insistence the point might never have been secured, especially as it had been turned down at all the three Conferences before and was negatived unequivocally even in the White Paper. This new safeguard, while beneficial to all the States as a body, will be of great value to the small States, as the additional seats thus available are likely to be placed at the disposal of the smaller States.

The claim of His Highness on the gratitude of the smaller States is increased by his unceasing advocacy of the admission into the Chamber of all States whose internal autonomy entitles them to that privilege. As is well known, the opinion of the Princes on the Standing Committee is not unanimous on this point, some of the rulers taking the view that any increase in the membership of the Chamber would lead to undesirable results. The Maharaja, on the other hand, always held that while the importance and authority of the larger States should be adequately recognized, the Chamber of Princes should give admission to all Rulers who can legitimately claim to be sovereign, and he emphasized this point in the meeting of the Special Committee held at Delhi on 25 March 1933. Later the Maharaja circulated a note of dissent on the subject, in the course of which it was stated:

'Out of over one hundred applicants, the Political Department, in their Memorandum, have recommended the inclusion of only twenty-one States, mainly on the basis of their population being over one lakh, and their revenue over three lakhs each. The majority of my colleagues do not favour the inclusion of such a number, for reasons which may be examined later. *I beg to differ on principle, and have, therefore, been reluctantly forced to record this dissent.*

'Under Article 2 of the Constitution of the Chamber of Princes, the Members of the Chamber shall be:

1. Rulers of States who enjoyed a dynastic salute of 11 guns or over on the 1st January 1921, and
2. Rulers of States who exercise such full or practically full internal powers as, in the opinion of the Viceroy, qualify them for admission to the Chamber.

'Prima facie, therefore, it seems that the right of Membership could not be denied to Rulers of States who exercise such full, or practically full, internal powers as, in the opinion of the Viceroy, qualify them for admission in the Chamber. The largeness of the number of the Indian States outside the Chamber has perforce suggested a limitation, as proposed by the Political Department, that new inclusions to the

Chamber be confined to States above a certain population and certain revenue. But once the existing restrictions on the powers of these twenty-one States are removed, in principle and in fairness and equity, their claim for inclusion becomes irresistible.'

In the same note His Highness made the following personal appeal to the Viceroy:

'that he may be pleased

1. to expedite the settlement of this question, and the consequent removal of restrictions on these States;
2. to consider sympathetically the question of the grant of gun salutes to these States in order to reconcile their position as Members of the Chamber, with their status; and
3. to examine sympathetically the claims of other States outside the Chamber who have not been recommended now for inclusion in the Chamber, by the accident of their population and revenue falling below the criterion now proposed for removal of restrictions on their powers.'

From the above summary it will be appreciated how profound and abiding is the interest that the Maharaja of Patiala has shown in furthering the claim of the smaller States; how, at the risk of unpopularity among Rulers of his own group and status, he has championed their cause; how, relegating his own interest to the background, he has fought for them, and how, during all his years of Chancellorship, His Highness has endeavoured to serve the cause of all, without fear or favour and with single-minded devotion to the interests of the entire Order of Princes.

CHAPTER V

THE PRINCES AND NATIONALISM

HIS HIGHNESS's first five-year period of Chancellorship synchronized with the development of the movement for the establishment of immediate Dominion Status for India. By 1926, when His Highness assumed the Chancellorship, the problem had acquired an immediacy which came as a surprise to many. But to the Maharaja, who had been studying the problem at close quarters, the importance that the problem assumed with the appointment of the Simon Commission seemed to be only natural. It was obvious that British India would be satisfied with nothing less than effective power at the centre and that the British Government would not for long resist such a demand which they themselves had on numerous occasions recognized to be reasonable. The interrelations of an Indian Government, responsible to the legislature, and the States whose paramountcy rested with the Crown, was a problem which alarmed the Princes by its implications, and puzzled British and Indian statesmen by its obvious complexities. What position would the Indian States occupy *vis-à-vis* an Indian Government in British India? Is British India entitled in any manner to exclusive authority in matters of common concern to States and British India? How will the problem of defence affect the treaty rights of the States? Would the rights claimed under paramountcy descend, so to say by inheritance, to British India? These were all problems which were new and unexplored at the time.

To appreciate fully the position at the time it is necessary to realize that even eminent jurists and constitutional thinkers like the late Lord Sinha, Sir Sivaswamy Aiyar, and the Rt. Hon. Sir Tej Bahadur Sapru had only vague notions about the status and rights of Indian States in a self-governing India. Sir Sivaswamy Aiyar at that time even went the length of denying that the relationship of the Indian States was with the Crown, and of holding that paramountcy was vested in the British-Indian Government. This was, in fact, the universally accepted view of Indian politicians and jurists. The danger to the future of the States was indeed very great. If British India acquired more power without a prior determination of the rights of the Indian States and a rigid definition of the relations between 'the two Indias', not only would paramountcy have passed into the hands of British Indians, but the economic and political interests of Indian States would have suffered serious encroachment. The history of the Montagu–Chelmsford Reforms provided sufficient proof of this tendency. The moment was indeed critical, and everything depended upon the Chancellor. The Chancellor recognized the seriousness of the position and with far-sighted statesmanship took the courageous step of initiating discussions with leading British-Indian statesmen. The steps taken by His Highness to determine the rights of the States and to establish their constitutional position in direct relationship with the British Crown have been detailed in a previous chapter. The step now taken by His Highness of trying to find a solution acceptable to British India and the States was a corollary to the appointment of the Butler Committee.

From the beginning the Maharaja of Patiala,

as Chancellor, did not conceal his conviction that India is entitled to the largest measure of self-government consistent with her position in the Empire. In a message given by his secretary to Reuter's representative at Bombay in 1928, His Highness stated:

'Moreover, the Indian States and British India live side by side in one great country which is rapidly becoming an economic whole, and unless they can co-operate in a fashion which will at once preserve the rights of either side and promote the welfare of all India, the future of the country, whatever its exact world position may be, must suffer.'

Again, in a speech at the East India Association on 23 July 1928, which was broadcast in England, His Highness said:

'Before I close, there are some few remarks which I should like to make. I want to emphasize most strongly, in the first place, that there is not, and cannot be, any ill will on the part of the Indian Princes towards the Nationalist movement in India. We Princes, like all the Nationalist leaders in British India, are firm believers in the value of the British connexion. We do believe, however, that it is perfectly compatible with that connexion that Indians should have greater power over the management of their own affairs than they possess to-day. We have not the slightest desire to thwart the progress of British India; indeed, we hope we shall run a friendly race with them along the lines of national development. For reasons which I have already indicated the States have some leeway to make up; but I should like to emphasize most strongly my belief that this leeway is not so great as is sometimes represented.'

It was in pursuance of this dual policy of ensuring the rights of the States and of supporting the legitimate claims of British India, that His Highness, in co-operation with his colleagues on the Standing Committee, initiated the policy of private discussions with British-Indian leaders. In 1930, after the meeting of the Chamber, His Highness invited prominent representatives of British-Indian opinion for an informal discussion and afterwards authorized Colonel K. N. Haksar and Sir Manubhai Mehta to keep in touch with them. The result of these discussions is well known. The idea of an All-India Federation as an effective solution of the Indian problems emerged from these discussions begun in Delhi and continued in London.

During the visit of the Statutory Commission

His Highness, as Chancellor, kept himself in close contact with the representatives of British and Indian opinion, and when it became clear that the Report of the Commission was unlikely to satisfy British India, in the same way that the Butler Report was unlikely to satisfy the States, His Highness was among the first to approve of the idea of the entire question being examined *de novo*. The representatives of the Chamber met Lord Irwin in Bombay in 1929 before his historic mission to England, and they represented that the solution of the Indian problem must take into consideration the rights of the Indian States; and when, on His Excellency's return, the announcement was made that H.M. Government had decided to call a Round Table Conference of the representatives of the Crown, British India, and the States, His Highness of Patiala was one of the first to welcome it. In a speech delivered at a banquet at Patiala immediately after the Viceroy's announcement, His Highness stated as follows:

'I am sure we all realize that we have reached a point in our lives where our responsibilities are exceptionally heavy. The situation that exists demands earnest and careful thought. The destiny of India as a whole, and therefore of the States of India, is trembling in the balance. The moment is pregnant with arresting potentialities. I feel, therefore, that you too would like me on this occasion to travel beyond the narrow circle of the complimentary utterance, and to express myself on a matter on which I am, perhaps, naturally and rightly expected to reveal my thoughts. So I propose to tell you the ideas that have occurred to me after perusing H.E. the Viceroy's recent pronouncement.

'I could have anticipated myself in this, and done so much earlier through the different vehicles of communication open to me, but I preferred to wait in order to give deep thought to that remarkable utterance.

'I realize that what I say would probably be read as coming from one who combines in himself a triple capacity, as the Ruler of Patiala, the Chancellor of the Chamber of Princes, and as a true friend of the British Government. These various capacities are in no sense exclusive; on the contrary they overlap and are intimately related with each other. In each and all of those capacities, I welcome His Excellency's pronouncement as timely and statesmanlike.

'Even as far as it goes—and it could not very well have gone farther—it announces a step, the essential first step, towards the ultimate solution of India's pressing constitutional problem.

'I say it, without hesitation and without fear of contradiction, that our Mother Country owes to Lord Irwin a deep debt for securing that there shall be a Round Table Conference between H.M. Government in England and all the different Indian interests. Our sense of gratitude to him is infinitely deepened when we realize, as we all should duly realize, the steadfastness of purpose, the sincerity of conviction, and the persuasive advocacy which His Excellency must have felt called upon to demonstrate, in the present condition of party politics in England, to enable himself to make such an announcement. And I would express the fervent hope that nothing further should occur to mar the very favourable effect which this pronouncement has already had in this country.

'Speaking as a patriotic Indian, I also venture to say that Lord Irwin has created a favourable opportunity for the early, honourable realization of India's legitimate political aspirations, through the only effective and the surest means of friendly negotiation. From the point of view of a Ruler, and of the Princes generally, I feel myself warranted in affirming that by ensuring the association of the Princes of India with the indispensable negotiations promised, he has done much to put heart into a body which, while remaining staunch to the British connexion, has not felt itself the gainer for its unflagging fidelity.

'He has created the possibility—no, I shall say he has ensured—that India's constitutional problem will be solved in a dignified manner and, let us hope, to the satisfaction of all parties concerned, and thus all such untoward developments would be averted as might have created insurmountable barriers between British and Indian India and might indeed have resulted in widespread and avoidable human suffering.

'I most earnestly trust that such a great opportunity will not be missed for the sake of mere sentiment, party gain, or personal prestige. The higher interest of the Motherland, I have no doubt, would be permitted to transcend all such ephemeral considerations. At the same time it is obvious that the maximum advantage can be derived from this unique opportunity only if we compose all our differences and go to the Conference truly united in heart and mind.

. . . . . .

'British India is asking for Dominion Status. I speak with due diffidence but, so far as I understand the matter, that phrase has not always carried the same rigidly defined connotation. It meant one thing before the Great War, it means something else to-day. Things evolve in the passage of time, they have to, they must be allowed to. Within the British Empire there are to-day various Dominions, each of which has a status of its own *vis-à-vis* the world and the Empire. India will have to have her own constitution. However analogous it may be, in the immediate future, to that of other Dominions, and however much it may, in due course, approach identity with any of them, as the conditions with us are our constitution will have to be somewhat different in direct relation to those conditions.

'The question arises:

'What should be the position of the States in the constitution that will come into being within the next year or two, and in the form it may assume at a later date? I have tried to answer this question to myself and I find that my thought is best expressed by Kipling's well-known verse:

> "Daughter am I in my Mother's house
> But mistress in my own."

This has been the insistent claim of the present generation of Indian Princes; it must be, it will be, the claim of the States *vis-à-vis* any Government of India.

'If it were necessary to make the position of myself and my brother Princes still clearer, I would recall the famous Resolution of the Imperial Conference of 1926, which reads:

'"Their position and mutual relation may be

readily defined. They are autonomous communities within the British Empire, equal in status, in no way subordinate one to another in any aspect of their domestic or external affairs, though united by a common allegiance to the Crown and freely associated as members of the British Commonwealth of Nations."

'If you want to get an approximate notion of the attitude of the States, all you have to do is to adapt this Resolution in the light of the history of the British connexion with the States, as enshrined in their subsisting Treaties. Eliminate "External Affairs", slightly qualify Equality of Status with due regard to factors that cannot be ignored, substitute for the "British Commonwealth of Nations" the "Federated States of India", and you have in a nut-shell what is more or less in the mind of the States, and an intensely earnest mind it is.

'This brings me to the question of Federation. This device has been suggested as the likeliest and the best solution of the Indian problem by many thinkers and endorsed as such by many political leaders in British India. They all have, however, insisted that over such a Federation should be superimposed a strong Central Government. It should be obvious that if the States are expected to consent to Federation, they cannot very well be left entirely outside that "Strong

Central Government", whatever form may be devised. It can only be introduced with their free and willing consent.'

Immediate action was required to determine the line to be followed by the Chancellor and the Standing Committee under the new circumstances, and at His Highness's suggestion the Special Organization was re-established with Colonel K. N. Haksar as Director. A comprehensive policy taking into consideration both the essential aspects of the question, viz. full safety for the rights of the States and increased political power for British India, had to be enunciated. The details of proposals had to be worked out, and their implications with regard to the sovereignty and rights of the States had to be examined; the opinions of the different groups of States and of the representatives of different interests had to be discovered and co-ordinated. Above all, it was essential to ensure that the entire body of States spoke with one united voice on this important occasion.

Adhering to his view that the prior determination of the rights of the States in relation to the Crown was necessary before a Federal or any other scheme could be devised, His Highness applied for another conference with the Viceroy. This meeting, which took place at Simla in July 1930, has been dealt with in another connexion. Here it is alluded to only in so far as it served as a preliminary step to the work of the Chamber at the Round Table Conference. For the first time the representatives of Hyderabad, Mysore, and Baroda also attended the meeting, and the general position of the States *vis-à-vis* British India was discussed with them.

In the middle of August His Highness left for England with a view to preparing the ground for pressing the point of view of the States at the Conference. The high esteem in which His Highness was held and the great impression that he created on the British public may be gauged by the fact that more than seventy-five members of Parliament belonging to all parties signed a letter of welcome in the following words:

'We the undersigned members of Parliament learn with much pleasure of your arrival in London and decision to take your place at the Round Table Conference.

'With sincere regret we have heard of your recent illness, and desire to express our hope that Your Highness may be speedily and completely restored to health.'

The signatories to this notable document included such well-known names as: R. C. Morrison, Wilfred Whiteley, Derwent Hall Caine, W. Hirst, Marion Phillips, Ian Macpherson, Eleanor Rathbone, Jack Jones, Edward Marjoribanks, Megan Lloyd George, George Dallas, Ben Turner, Holford Knight, and Norman Angell.

When the Round Table Conference was opened by His late Majesty at the House of Lords, it fell to His Highness, as Chancellor, to propose in a short speech that Mr. Ramsay MacDonald, as Prime Minister, should preside at the Conference. His Highness was the leader of the Indian States Delegation, and in that capacity was responsible for the extraordinarily cordial relations that prevailed between the representatives of British India and the Indian States. Through the Director of the Special Organization he kept himself in close touch with all British-Indian parties, and was thus able to exert his influence without entering into the details of party politics.

It is thus due to the Maharaja of Patiala's initiative and statesmanship that the wise policy of close consultation between Indian States and British India was inaugurated; that a progressive and forward policy was officially adopted by the Chamber in regard to the claim of British India for self-government, while insisting strongly and unbendingly on the just and legitimate rights of the States. The summoning of the Round Table Conference, the subsequent history of the co-operation between British India and the Indian States in the framing of a Federal Constitution with central responsibility, and the prospect of an honourable settlement between the Crown, British India, and the States are but the outcome of that wise policy. And since His Highness's reassumption of the duties of Chancellorship in 1933 he has with equal courage and frankness emphasized that policy, as will be evident from the following statement issued to the Press by His Highness at Bombay:

'I propose to devote my mind and best efforts towards the triumphant emergence of India from a state of dependency towards a great self-governing dominion of His Majesty. We do not come into the Federation to dominate British India, but our object is to guide it to the path of glory and success by our co-operation.

'While we are insistent on preserving our relations with the Crown, and are equally insistent upon our internal autonomy and independence, we are equally jealous of the rights of British Indians in the Commonwealth of Nations. We propose to work in harmonious co-operation with the representatives of the Crown and British India. I am sure we are all as determined as His Majesty's Government not to throw away the labours spent on evolving a constitution for India on Federal lines which we accepted at the invitation of British Indian leaders to secure responsibility at the Centre.'

His Highness's Chancellorship may thus be said to have laid the foundation of Greater India—an India in which the States, as equal and autonomous entities, will take their due share in the Government of a free and federated Dominion.

CHAPTER VI

CONSTITUTIONAL CHANGES IN THE CHAMBER

THE position of the Chamber of Princes when H.H. the Maharaja of Patiala took office as Chancellor may be judged from the fact that, though the Standing Committee was the representative body of Princes, it was the Political Secretary and not the Chancellor who presided over the discussions of the Committee. Even when it was considered desirable that a Prince should preside, the selection was made *ad hoc*. In fact, when His Highness assumed charge, the Chancellor's position was undefined, and the representative character of his office unrecognized. Again, while the Political Secretary had the benefit of his expert advisers, the Princes were not allowed to take any Ministers to the Standing Committee.

No meetings of the Standing Committee without the presence of the Political Secretary were ever held, and the informal Conferences of Princes and Ministers which precede the Annual Chamber Session were still in their infancy. There was neither any regular procedure nor any important business transacted in those Conferences.

Above all, the agenda of the Chamber and the Standing Committee was framed by the Political Secretary for the approval of the Viceroy, and neither the Chancellor nor the Standing Committee were ever consulted.

In actual fact, at the time that His Highness assumed office the functions and authority of the Chancellor were left fluid; his position in relation even to the Standing Committee and *vis-à-vis* the Political Department had not become established. The Chancellorship was still a new office, and it was chiefly due to the personality of the first Chancellor that the Chamber became effective at all.

This is a part of the unique achievements of H.H. the Maharaja of Bikaner, who, as General Secretary and later as Chancellor, directed the affairs of the Chamber in its early days. The organization of a new institution is always difficult; but it is doubly so when that organization is composed of Princes who have had no experience in collective work.

The first five-year Chancellorship of His Highness of Patiala changed all this. When His Highness handed over charge to His Highness of Bhopal the cash transferred amounted to Rs. 5 lakhs. A proper, permanent Secretariat was created for the Chancellor. From small beginnings the Secretariat grew during His Highness's régime into a big department, able to deal with all the technical points arising either out of the work of the Chamber or from the references from individual States. Apart from the work which the Chancellor did himself, a great deal of work was done in the Central Secretariat by way of preparation of notes on all important questions, examination of new questions for negotiations with the Political Department, co-ordination of the meetings of Ministers, and opinion on technical issues raised by other States. The establishment of a proper Secretariat, originally paid for by His Highness personally out of the revenues of his State and later on as an independent office, was a reform of great importance, as it enabled the Princes to go to the meetings with the Political Secretary, with their side of the case fully prepared. Without such an organization, which His Highness established at the very commencement of his Chancellorship, the changes in the constitutional procedure which His Highness was later on able to introduce would not have been possible. The Chamber section of the Ijlas-i-Khas Office at Patiala before the office was separated shouldered very heavy responsibility and is entitled to the gratitude of the Princes.

The formal meetings of the Standing Committee used previously to be conducted by the Political Secretary. His Highness considered this to be irregular and against the prestige of the Chancellor, and the position has since been changed. Now the Political Secretary attends the Standing Committee meetings more in order to explain the position of the Government and generally to discuss with the Standing Committee the questions at issue. The views of the Standing Committee are generally put forward by the Chancellor, who, having discussed them previously with his colleagues, acts as their spokesman.

Another important reform for which His Highness was responsible was an amendment of the rules by which the presence of the Chancellor's Secretary was made compulsory at the meetings of the Standing Committee. Originally only the Princes and the Political Secretary used to be present at these meetings. This placed the Princes at a great disadvantage in their negotiations with the Political Secretary, who had ready at his elbow the necessary files on all questions and further had the benefit of expert advisers. The Princes, on the other hand, apart from being handicapped by their lack of familiarity with legal and other technical questions, had neither a Secretariat nor expert advisers when they met the Political Secretary. His Highness therefore pressed that his Secretary and other experts should be present at the meetings, and the rule was accordingly altered by which, apart from advisers and experts, it was laid down that the Secretary to the Chancellor should invariably be present at all meetings of the Standing Committee and should be allowed to speak when invited to do so.

The informal meeting of the Standing Committee, which has now become a regular feature of the work of the Chamber, is another important innovation introduced by His Highness. Before 1926 the Standing Committee only used to meet formally in the presence of the Political Secretary. Much inconvenience was felt by the Princes, as this procedure did not enable them to discuss among themselves, or take up questions with which the Government of India was not concerned, at least in the preliminary stages. His Highness first invited the Princes on the Standing Committee for a private meeting at Simla in September 1926. The establishment of a Secretariat helped to give it a regular position, enabling proper record of discussions and decisions to be kept. From that time it became the custom for the Standing Committee to meet at convenient places, and formulate their views on all important questions. Slowly it assumed a formal character, and its decisions were attended to, and often its opinions invited, by the Government of India. In fact, though still called informal, its proceedings are circulated and approved by the Standing Committee, and on points of difficulty like the attendance of substitute members the decision of His Excellency is taken and followed. The establishment of the informal meetings of the Standing Committee has had the result of transferring to it much of the preliminary work which used to be done in the presence of the Political Secretary, and has further improved the status of the Chancellor, as, when he writes or speaks to the Political Secretary, he does so on behalf and in the name of the Standing Committee.

The informal Conference of Princes which precedes the annual session of the Chamber also changed in its character during the Chancellorship of His Highness of Patiala. At the first informal meeting held during His Highness's Chancellorship, it is interesting to note, it was not the Chancellor who presided but H.H. the Maharaja of Bikaner. In this matter a new procedure was introduced by which the Chancellor was in future to preside at all informal meetings.

His Highness also initiated the system of having the discussions at the informal conferences on the basis of notes and memoranda prepared for the occasion. This had the advantage of directing discussions to relevant subjects, the material for which was prepared and placed before the meeting. His Highness himself started the discussions on these questions, and placed before the Conference a report of the work done by him on many subjects of importance. For the first time systematic and audited accounts were also placed before the Conference. During the fifth year of His Highness's régime the Maharaja further improved the procedure by deciding that regular rules for the conduct of business should be drafted and passed, and the work of the Conference should be conducted in accordance with a defined procedure.

In regard also to the procedure in the Chamber His Highness's Chancellorship saw important changes. Previously the sessions of the Chamber were held in secret. The result was that many misunderstandings arose about the nature of the work and the Princes therefore considered that it was wiser to hold the sessions in public, reserving only the right to hold private sessions whenever occasion might necessitate this. A more important change, which also was introduced in the time of His Highness's Chancellorship, was in regard to the agenda of the Chamber, which used to be prepared by the Political Secretary in consultation with the Viceroy. This was felt to be an unnecessary restriction, and a resolution was adopted in the Chamber giving to the Standing Committee the right of framing the agenda, subject to the approval of H.E. the Viceroy.

The cumulative effect of all these changes was to convert the Chancellor from an official into an authorized spokesman of the Princes, in relation to the Viceroy and the Political Department. The change in the position is evidenced by the fact that on all important public questions like the work in regard to the Butler Committee, the action to be taken on their Report, &c., the Chancellor effectively moulded the opinion of the Princes. In one year alone His Highness issued thirty-two circular letters calling attention to various points and bringing together the points of view of the States. Backed by such support, it was possible for the Chancellor to approach the Viceroy and the Political Department as the official spokesman of the Princes, a claim which no one was in a position to contest or deny.

The Standing Committee also increased in prestige and authority. It became the elected executive of the Chamber, the authorized representative of the general body of Princes. When their informal meetings gained semi-official recognition, the Standing Committee was able to stand forth as a united body whose duty it was to look after and champion the interest of the Princes as a whole. The original purpose of negotiations on the twenty-three points fell more and more into the background, and gave place to the discussion of main lines of policy. When the entire Standing Committee was, at His Highness's suggestion, selected by Lord Irwin to represent the Princes at the Round Table Conference, it may well be said that its character as the authorized executive of the Chamber received official recognition.

These important constitutional changes, which transformed the Chamber of Princes into an effective political institution within a short period of five years, were not brought about without heavy expenditure of money, and great and sustained effort. Assisted by a body of efficient advisers and experts of recognized ability, His Highness devoted a great deal of his time to this important work. True, funds were generously subscribed by other Princes, but the share of expenditure which fell on the Patiala treasury during these five years, without taking into consideration the expenditure incurred by His Highness on his visit to Europe for the Butler Committee, is estimated at not less than Rs. 10 lakhs. Thus it was at the sacrifice of a great deal of money and at great personal inconvenience that His Highness carried on this noble work in the service of his Order.

CHAPTER VII

SAFEGUARDING THE STATES

UNGENEROUS critics have often attacked the Maharaja of Patiala on the ground of his inconsistency in regard to the Federation. They have said that his public professions have not always been in conformity with his private activities; that while declaring himself to be in favour of Federation, he was all the time interested in wrecking it; that he missed no opportunity of organizing opposition and of allying himself with every element in British and Indian politics inimical to the Federal scheme. It is perfectly true that the opinion of the Maharaja underwent very considerable modification during the course of the last six years. Indeed, it would have been surprising if it had not done so. Not one of the many distinguished statesmen, lawyers, and politicians who attended the first Round Table Conference and enthusiastically supported the idea of Federation had any precise idea of the details of a Federal Constitution for India. Federation, at the first Round

Table Conference, was merely an ideal, a generous and warm-hearted, though nebulous, expression of the agelong desire of India for unity. Not even the most far-sighted could foresee what form the ideal would take when translated into a constitutional scheme. The changes and transformations of political opinion consequent upon the elaboration of the Federal ideal may be illustrated by the reflection that a statesman who objected vigorously to the scheme in 1930, yet four years later, as Secretary-of-State, piloted the Bill with extraordinary ability through the House of Commons.

After the emotionalism of 1930 there was undoubtedly a reaction. The Maharaja, as the spokesman of a large body of Princes, began to feel that the acceptance of the Federal scheme was perhaps too unqualified, and that in the enthusiasm of the moment no effort was made to give detailed consideration to the vital questions affecting the sovereignty and privileges of the States. Critical examination, undertaken at leisure, also revealed a number of important defects in the scheme, to which His Highness, though not Chancellor at the time, felt it his duty to call attention. At the risk of being misunderstood and abused, His Highness declared for a re-examination of the whole scheme.

The breach in the ranks of the Princes was fortunately short-lived. Their Highnesses of Bikaner and Bhopal, who were the leaders of what was then called the pro-Federation section, realized that the views which the Maharaja of Patiala urged could not be set aside, as they represented a very powerful body of opinion in the Chamber of Princes. His Highness also recognized that only through united action could the interests of the States be fully secured and their rights safeguarded. Accordingly, at His Highness's invitation, a meeting was arranged with Their Highnesses of Bikaner and Bhopal on the 11th of March 1932, and a representative Committee of Ministers was appointed to advise Their Highnesses on the constitutional problems before them.

The Committee, of which Sir C. P. Ramaswamy Aiyar was President, included Sir Akbar Hydari, Sir Prabhashankar Pattani, Sir Manubhai Mehta, Colonel Kailas Haksar, the Yuvraj of Limbdi, and Sardar K. M. Panikkar. This

Committee submitted a Report which recommended the acceptance of the Federal scheme subject to the condition that the safeguards which the Committee drew up as being essential for the maintenance of the rights of the States were provided for in the scheme. This historic Report became the basis of the Delhi Pact (March 1932) by which unity among the leading Princes on the question of Federation was finally achieved.

Speaking in regard to the work of this Committee, His Highness, in a statement made before the informal meeting of the Princes on 25 March 1932, said:

> 'Luckily, the foundations of the much-needed understanding and unity have been substantially laid, and we meet to-day not as partisans, but as a band of united workers and brothers determined to subordinate all personal and party tags to the well-being of our Order and of the States.'

It was not to be expected that on so complicated a question as the relation of Indian States to the proposed Federation of India complete unanimity could be achieved among so individualistic a body as the Chamber of Princes.

Therefore it is no small achievement that through the Maharaja of Patiala's efforts substantial unity was brought about among the leading Princes of India. It became thereafter possible for the united voice of the Princes to be heard on important issues affecting them. No longer divided and disunited, they were able to pull their weight in the discussions that followed. The Government in England knew what it was that the Princes considered as their minimum demands; the States were equally made aware as to what it was that Federation involved. In fact, the Delhi Pact meant the crystallization of opinion with regard to the Federal schemes.

It is a remarkable tribute to the wisdom of the Ministers who worked out that Report that practically every one of the conditions which they laid down as essential has been incorporated in the Act. Besides, the unity which the Report brought about gave to the voice of the Princes a weight, and secured for their views full and adequate consideration from H.M. Government.

As a result of the agreement reached, the

following resolution was proposed and adopted by the Chamber of Princes:

'This Chamber declares that the States will join an All-India Federation on the assumption that the Crown will accept responsibility for securing to them the following guarantees:

a. that the necessary safeguards will be embodied in the Constitution;

b. that under the Constitution, their rights arising from Treaties, or Sanads or Engagements, remain inviolate and inviolable;

c. that the sovereignty and internal independence of the States remain intact and are preserved and fully respected and stated that the obligations of the Crown to the States remain unaltered.'

Seconding this resolution the Maharaja of Patiala said:

'The Indian Princes, Sir, recognize that they owe triple obligations to the Crown, to their States, and to India. As such any scheme, worthy of their support and participation, must ensure simultaneous and effective discharge of these triple obligations. This is the proviso, with which we all conditioned our support to the principle of Federation when we met at the first Round Table Conference. The working out of a Federal Scheme, embodying the suggestions of the different interests involved, consistent with a composite and workable constitution for Greater India, was referred to the Federal Structure Committee. The Committee produced a scheme, and be it said to their credit that they laboured hard, and that their scheme, which in their own words was only a skeleton to be filled in, provoked constructive thought and brought out the main issues involved. Some of us, on a leisured and closer examination of the scheme as it stood, felt that it did not completely fulfil the tests under which we could safely come into it, capable of effectively discharging our treaty obligations to the Crown, to our States, and to India. Those of us who felt that way had a very delicate and difficult task to perform. Our silence would have meant that the scheme would have proceeded on those lines, and necessary safeguards would not have been pressed for incorporation which alone could make it acceptable to the majority of the Indian States; and we would have been faced with a dilemma, when the picture was completed, of the Princes refusing their adherence. An open expression of views, on the other hand, was likely to excite misunderstandings and misgivings, both amongst the advocates of the Sankey Scheme and in British India. We anxiously weighed all these; and finally decided in the interests of the States, of India and the Empire, to declare what we felt. Our intentions were misunderstood; our motives were misrepresented. This was not unexpected. But we were convinced that when our various suggestions should be dispassionately examined no true friend of the States amongst the Princes would be able to afford to stand apart . . . and I am happy to be able to declare, unequivocally, that we all stand united on the fundamental essentials involved. We have ceased to represent different parties and groups on the main planks of an All-India Constitution. Our united programme is embodied in this and the next Resolution.'

The work which had been begun by the signing of the Delhi Pact was resumed by His Highness when he was again elected Chancellor (April 1933). The problem that faced His Highness as Chancellor was not too easy. After prolonged discussions at three Round Table Conferences, His Majesty's Government had formulated their specific proposals in a White Paper, which was to be subjected to the examination of a Joint Select Committee of the two Houses of Parliament. On a close examination of the White Paper proposals, it was found that some of the safeguards formulated by the Princes at Delhi had not been provided for. It was necessary to send a delegation to England with instructions to secure those points which had been omitted. So again Sir Manubhai Mehta and Nawab Sir Liaqat Hyat Khan were sent as delegates to the Joint Select Committee, and Mr. Mahbool Mahmood and Sardar K. M. Panikkar were sent to advise them.

After communicating the list of the essential safeguards, the Maharaja laid down the instructions:

'These are the essential safeguards which the Standing Committee as at present advised insist upon as *sine qua non* for their entry into the Federation. The Princes on the Standing Committee desire that you should strictly adhere to the terms laid down and should under no conditions yield on your own responsibility to any subtraction from or limitations to these conditions. If political or other considerations render it inadvisable or inexpedient to press for any one of these, or you are satisfied that it is impossible to obtain satisfaction on any particular point, immediate reference should be made by code telegram to the Chancellor who will communicate with the Standing Committee.'

One of the most important questions connected with the entry of the States into Federation was the consideration of the list of the Federal subjects. While the Princes' delegates to the Joint Parliamentary Committee were, in accordance with the instructions given to them by the Chancellor on behalf of the Standing Committee, engaged upon securing the incorporation, in the recommendations of that Committee, of the conditions and safeguards considered as essential by the Indian States, His Highness, as Chancellor, convened a meeting of the Standing Committee at Bombay in June 1933 to discuss this list of Federal subjects and to send instructions accordingly to the Ministers at the Joint Parliamentary Committee.

In November 1934 the Report of the Joint Parliamentary Committee was published. It was quite clear that this Report represented the final views of the British Government in regard to constitutional reforms. In fact it was the *completed picture* for which the Princes were waiting. It was announced that the Government of India Bill would not be materially different from the Report. It became, therefore, most necessary that the Joint Parliamentary Committee's Report and the Bill should be subjected to the closest scrutiny and examination from the legal point of view by eminent Counsel, and from the administrative point of view by the Ministers. His Highness had foreseen this necessity and engaged the services of Mr. Wilfrid Greene, K.C., Professor J. H. Morgan, K.C., and Mr. Lennox McNair. For the examination of the Report from the administrative and other points of view the Maharaja, along with the Rulers of Bikaner and Bhopal, had constituted an informal committee of the most prominent Ministers. This Committee consisted, among others, of the Rt. Hon. Sir Akbar Hydari, Sir V. T. Kishnama Chari (Baroda), Sir Mirza Ismail (Mysore), Sir Manubhai Mehta (Bikaner), Sir C. P. Ramaswamy Aiyar (Travancore), Sir Kailas Haksar (Gwalior), Sir Liaqat Hyat Khan (Patiala), Sir S. M. Bapna (Indore), Sardar K. M. Panikkar (Patiala), Sir Prabhashankar Pattani (Bhavanagar), K. A. H. Abbassi (Bhopal), Col. E. J. D. Colvin (Kashmir), with Mr. K. C. Neogy and Mr. D. K. Sen to represent the smaller States. This Committee may fairly be said to speak for the entire body of Indian States, both by the wealth of its talent and the representative character of its Ministers.

Before the examination of the Joint Parliamentary Committee Report by Counsel and by Ministers could be completed, the Annual Session of the Chamber was summoned (21 to 24 January 1935). The Maharaja, as Chancellor, felt that the collective views of the Princes could best be expressed at a specially summoned meeting away from the official capital. It was, however, necessary to reaffirm the reservations, and the Chamber therefore adopted the following resolution, which was moved by the Maharaja in a speech which was justly recognized as an epoch-making utterance.

The resolution which was passed at the meeting in regard to the question of the States' entry into the Federation is here quoted:

1. The Chamber of Princes reaffirms its previous declaration about the readiness of the States to accede to an All-India Federation, provided that the essential conditions and guarantee which have been pressed for are included in the constitution.
2. The Chamber must, however, reserve its opinion on the question until the Parliamentary Bill

relating to the Constitutional Reforms and the contents of the proposed Treaty of Accession and of the Instrument of Instructions to the Viceroy are known and have been examined.

3. The Chamber also wishes to emphasize that the inauguration and success of federation will depend entirely on the goodwill and co-operation of all the parties concerned, and upon the clear recognition of the Sovereignty of the States and of their rights under Treaties and engagements.

4. The Chamber further emphasizes the necessity of the prior settlement of the pending claims of individual States.

Realizing that it was perhaps the last occasion in which the collective voice of the Princes would be heard on this question, the Maharaja asked for calm consideration of the problem, in view not only of its amazing complexity, but also of the fundamental character of the change which the Federal Constitution would introduce into the political life of the States.

'Let us not forget', he said, 'that the change that is suggested, whether beneficial or otherwise, is of a most momentous character. It would undoubtedly involve a fundamental change in our relations with British India. From politically separate entities in all matters, the States under a federation will become politically united with British India in certain specified matters. Common institutions, common policies, common responsibilities will arise which in the federal field will unite the States and British India into one whole. No one would deny that these are fundamental changes at which the most courageous and stout-hearted champions of the proposals may feel legitimate qualms, while others to whom federation was no more than an idea will undoubtedly feel alarm and anxiety.'

He warned them of the financial liabilities that might follow, of the possibility of the encroachment by the Central Government on the authority of the States. His Highness said:

'Nor are we entitled to forget that this Government of a United India once established will grow and continue to grow in a manner which we cannot foresee now. No institution devised by man develops exactly as its originator intends; least of all a constitution which vests great power and gives legal, executive and judicial authority, no doubt in specified matters, over a whole country. Unforeseen conditions develop; circumstances not contemplated at the present time come into being and the Federal Government may be forced, even if it were unwilling, to expand its functions and even its scope. We have the example of the United States, and even of Imperial Germany, to show that even when States' rights were rigorously and almost religiously safeguarded in the Constitution, the central governments have inevitably encroached on the powers of the constituent units.'

The momentous character of the decision which the Princes would have to take, the finality, the irretrievability of such a decision, the consequences which might follow from it, made him keenly alive to his own overwhelming responsibility as leader of the Princely Order. No one was enthusiastic about the scheme, which, like all political contrivances, was the result of compromise and adjustment. The Princes most friendly to the scheme merely harped on its inevitability, on the decision of the Government of India to put the scheme through at all costs. It would have been easy for the Maharaja of Patiala also to take that line. He would have remained popular with the Government and its officials, who would have seen in his every action further evidence of high statesmanship. But on such an occasion as this, when the future, indeed the existence, of the States was in question, the Maharaja refused to be a trimmer. He appealed to the Princes to consider every aspect of the question before making a decision; warned British India firmly against any coercion of the States contrary to their interests, reminded the Crown of its obligation to maintain inviolate the rights and prerogatives of the States.

The concluding portion of this speech, which for the first time boldly placed before the world the candid view of the Princes, is so important for an understanding of His Highness's mind (and the events that followed at Bombay) that it is quoted in full as Appendix IV, and for convenience some extracts are given here:

'The circumstances under which some of us agreed to consider a Federal proposal, as providing a suitable scheme of co-operation between British India and the States, are indeed well known. It was not from any desire on our part to hinder British India in the realization of its legitimate aspirations, but rather to help India in her constitutional progress and political development, without sacrificing our own sovereignty and internal autonomy; but to-day responsible men in British India, men who I know bear no ill will towards the States, have not hesitated to say frankly that in the present scheme of things, Indian States have become a positive hindrance rather than help to British India. I would not have taken such an expression of views from however eminent a quarter seriously but for the fact that it seems to be widely held in all sections of political opinion in British India. And if that is the view of men of moderation in the country, it is a matter for Your Highnesses seriously to consider whether we should put ourselves in the position in which practically every important body of opinion in British India considers us unwelcome partners, and looks upon our entry into Federation with suspicion. The benefits of a Federal scheme to the Indian States are in any case not so overwhelming that, whatever the opinion of British India, it would be in our interest to join it. On the other hand, if, as it would seem, the invitation of British India, which we willingly accepted, does not stand, and the benefits to the States are not obvious, the Princes for their part should be prepared to say that while they are willing, as they have always been, to enter into a federation, they would be equally prepared to stand out of a Federal scheme if British India is not anxious to have it. In view of the accusation that is being levelled against the States, I think it is necessary that our views should be clearly and unequivocally stated on this issue. . . .

'It is well to clear all misconceptions. If the Princes

decide to enter the Federation, they will do so with their eyes open, with the firm determination to cultivate feelings of friendship with British India, and co-operate with them in all matters concerning the welfare of this great country. But they will under no circumstances permit the utilization of the constitution for interference between themselves and their people. It must be clearly understood that the Princes will accept no constitution which would even by implication vest in any authority except themselves the right to decide their relations with their own people, the right to modify or alter their own polities, their right to live in the manner they and their people choose.

'If, however, the critics of the States have in their mind the belief that they could assume political power in India, without taking into consideration the claims of the States and the just rights of the Princes, I would in all friendliness but with all firmness say that such a course would never be acceptable to the States. The sovereign rights, prerogatives, and privileges of the States are inherent in them and are guaranteed by solemn treaties. The Crown is under the most sacred obligation to keep them inviolate and inviolable, and there is no authority which can in any manner and at any time encroach upon them or question their validity. The idea that the States and their Rulers are an anachronism in the political life of India to-day, that they are merely apocryphal passages in the history of India, interpolated by a Machiavellian hand, which could be torn away without affecting the whole, is so utterly unhistorical as to require no comment. If British India desires to gc forward without the association of the States, we shall have no complaint. The States of India stand by their own internal strength, by the loyalty of their people to their Rulers, by the bond of affection anc attachment which unites the Princes and their people They are rooted in age-long history and I have the faith in me that federation or no federation, the State of India will exist as integral parts in the polity of thi great country, so long as the Rulers are true to thei tradition of *Raj Dharma* and to their trust.

'Your Highnesses, I confess I am an optimist. have firm faith in the future of our States and of ou Order. If British India is prepared for a Federal con stitution, and that constitution assures us our rights o internal sovereignty, does not weaken the ties tha bind us to our people and the Crown, secures to u our essential terms and does not impose unbearable burdens on our finance, we shall, as we have always said, join it. But, let me say it most emphatically, we are not enamoured of a Federal constitution as such; we have never approached His Majesty's Government and requested them to devise a federal constitution in order to safeguard our future. If the Crown and British India, as the other parties to the constitutional development of India, desire the establishment of a federal constitution, we for our part will be prepared to consider it sympathetically and with every desire not to stand in the way of the attainment by India of its status.'

This speech, with its uncompromising formulation of the Princes' claims and its independent attitude towards the Federal proposals, created a stir in Government circles. The Chancellor was accused of attempting to wreck the scheme; his speech was described as an act of wanton sabotage. The claims of the States were pooh-poohed; the inevitability of the scheme, whatever its provisions, was again asserted. In fact, the attitude of the Government of India was that the only right that the Princes had was to sing in chorus praising the wisdom of the Government's decision—whatever that decision might be. The Maharaja of Patiala was not agreeable to that view. He said: 'I will advise the Princes to join the Federation provided our conditions are satisfied. If the conditions are not satisfied you must not assume that we shall follow with docility what you decide for us.' Naturally the authorities were angry.

The day after the session of the Chamber of Princes the draft India Bill was published. An intimation was sent to the Chancellor that any criticism that the Princes had to offer should be sent within twenty days. The Maharaja felt that this was an attempt to rush the Princes blindfold, without even giving them an opportunity to examine the Bill, and protested strongly to this effect in a cabled communication to the Secretary-of-State. As a result of this pressure the Secretary-of-State reluctantly agreed to the time being extended to the end of February.

The technical examination of the Bill was, in the meantime, being carried on by the Ministers' Committee. But the Chancellor felt that the Princes themselves should express their views unequivocally at this stage, if their interests were to be fully safeguarded. With this object he called an informal meeting of Princes and Ministers at Bombay on 25 February 1935. This meeting, which is one of the most historic gatherings of the Princes, took place in the Patiala

House at Bombay, and was attended by about twenty-six Rulers, including the Maharajas of Bikaner, Rewa, Dholpur, and Dewas Junior, and over sixty Ministers. It was clear from the beginning that the draft Bill was in many important respects unacceptable to the Princes. It was felt, not only by those Princes and Ministers who had always opposed the Federal scheme, but even by men like Sir Akbar Hydari and Sir C. P. Ramaswamy Aiyar, that the Bill did not implement many of the undertakings given to the Princes by H.M. Government, and that in some other cases the provisions of the Bill introduced principles which had not been discussed at all. Feeling ran high, and the speeches delivered even by the friends of the Federation were of a kind that had never been heard before in any conference of Princes.

Unfortunately the whole proceedings, including the shorthand report of the speeches, leaked out in the press, and provided Mr. Winston Churchill with unexpected powder and shot for a frontal attack on the Bill. The intention of the Chancellor was not to kill the reforms, but merely to secure the amendments which the

Princes considered necessary. But the die-hard opposition in England took a totally different view of the proceedings, and for a day or two, till the excitement of the meeting died down and the real meaning of the Princes' action became clear, the Bill itself was temporarily in danger.

The true inwardness of the Princes' criticism was made clear by the joint letter which the Chancellor and the Rulers of Bikaner and Bhopal addressed to the Viceroy. That letter, which was printed as a part of the White Paper on the Princes' claims, pointed out the changes which were required to make the Bill acceptable to the Princes. In the face of that letter the criticism that was widely expressed, that the Chancellor was bent on wrecking the scheme at all costs, lost its point. It became clear that the only interest that he had was to safeguard the interests of the States, which as their elected Chancellor he was in duty bound to do.

The abuse to which the Maharaja was subjected for this courageous action was the penalty he had to pay for fighting the cause of the Princes.

The Secretary-of-State, on being apprised of the situation, expressed his willingness to introduce amendments to meet the point of view of the Princes, and the Chancellor immediately deputed Sir Liaqat Hyat Khan, Sir Manubhai Mehta, Sardar K. M. Panikkar, and Mr. D. K. Sen to proceed to England and instruct Counsel in these negotiations. Mr. Wilfrid Greene, K.C., and Mr. McNair, who had been retained for the Chamber, set to work immediately, and through their valuable efforts the Princes were able to secure the substance of every amendment which had been suggested by the Bombay Conference. This object was not achieved without very considerable expenditure by, and much inconvenience to, His Highness personally. The Chamber had not sufficient funds to pay the expenses of the Ministers and of Counsel. Money had to be advanced as a loan to the Chamber from the Patiala State. The Standing Committee, till the last minute, failed to recognize the importance of these negotiations, and a powerful group within the Committee hesitated to give authority to the Chancellor to carry on these negotiations in England. And yet, under his instructions and on his responsibility, the work was carried forward, and no less than forty amendments in the interests of the Princes were introduced and carried in Parliament—indeed a unique record of success in the face of the most difficult circumstances.

The action which he took brought him into conflict with the authorities, who did not at first recognize the fact that, when changes of such momentous character are involved, the elected spokesman of a privileged Order has the solemn duty of doing everything in his power to safeguard the interests of those who have put their trust in him. But who will now deny that the Bombay meeting and the resolution passed at the Maharaja's insistence constituted a turning-point in the negotiations regarding Federation, since they led to a modification of the scheme in many respects, which, without altering the structure of the Bill, provided the safeguards necessary for the entry of the States into the Federation?

From what has been said in the foregoing pages, it should be apparent that the Chancellorship of H.H. the Maharaja of Patiala has been, from every point of view, a period of significance for the Princes and States of India; that His Highness, by placing his great ability and talent, the prestige and authority which he enjoys as the Ruler of the premier State in the Punjab, and the resources of his State at the disposal of his Order, served their interests and achieved unique results; that he has safeguarded by every method available to him the rights and privileges of all States; that he has fought with unflinching courage for the recovery of their authority and dignity; that he has succeeded in improving the constitutional position of the smaller States, and in securing to them a position which they had not enjoyed before; that he has brought about changes in the constitution and working of the Chamber which have converted it into an effective organ of princely opinion. Further, it has been shown that in all this work, connected essentially though it was with the special rights of the States, His Highness kept the wider interests of India at heart and supported in every way the claim of British India for increased political power. Thus, viewed from every standpoint, His Highness's nine years of Chancellorship will stand out in modern Indian history as a period of great achievement, of which the Princes as a whole and H.H. the Maharaja of Patiala may justly be proud.

APPENDIX I

AIDE-MÉMOIRE FOR THE VICEROY (1927)

We have been taking stock of our position in view of the approach of the Royal Commission upon Constitutional Reforms in British India. We do not venture to prophesy whether this Commission will be followed by a further instalment of Reforms; but it is a contingency which cannot be ignored. The result of our stock-taking has been an increased realization of the fact that our position, during the last twelve years of intensive development in British India, has been adversely affected to a degree not generally appreciated. It is true that the Princes' Conference or its successor, the Chamber of Princes, has been functioning through much of this period with the object of affording us an opportunity of maintaining and improving our position. Yet we are convinced that on the whole that position is marked by steady weakening in a variety of directions, both political and economic. We are therefore convinced of the necessity of an immediate investigation of the position prior to the appointment of the Royal Commission for British India. Such investigation could only be satisfactorily undertaken jointly by ourselves and our Ministers on the one hand, and on the other by impartial and independent men to be nominated by mutual consent of ourselves and the Government of India.

2. Ingeneral we desire that means should be devised for safeguarding our position in respect of—

(*a*) the internal autonomy of our States, and

(*b*) those vital interests, economic and fiscal, which in the past years have been adversely affected.

3. In particular we put forward the following requests:

1. *That the Government of India should admit the full consequences of the true legal position of the States by recognizing that the Governor-General-in-Council is not the final authority in regard to them.*

(EXPLANATION.)

The Government of India under the present constitution, is subject to the 'direction, control and superintendence of the Secretary of State', who, being an integral part of the Governance of India, is the final authority, subject to the British Parliament.

2. *That when, in consequence of further devolution of Power from England to India, either the functions and authority of the Secretary-of-State are curtailed, or the Government of India becomes responsible to the people of British India, the right of the States in the one case to appeal against the decisions of the Governor-General-in-Council, or in the other case to secure the impartial adjustment of conflicts of interest between themselves and British India, shall be safeguarded by the creation of statutory machinery competent to adjudicate between the parties.*

(EXPLANATION.)

A safeguarding provision should be included in the Government of India Act to be passed by Parliament, providing for the creation of machinery to adjudicate between the States and the future Government of India. This will entail the execution of a Covenant between the future Government of India and the States, which must be ratified by Parliament and further supplemented by suitable directions in the Instruments of Instruction to the Heads of the Central and Provincial Governments. Thus such covenants will be parts of the Indian Constitution and a permanent security to the States.

Provided that in cases involving the personal conduct of a Ruling Prince, the Crown alone could be appealed to by the successors of the present Government of India; for it is obvious that when the change in the powers of the Government of India, as set forth above, occurs, that Government could not act upon the basic formula which in such matters governs the rights of the Paramount Power to intervene.

3. *That the recommendations contained in paragraph 302 of the Montagu–Chelmsford Report should be fully implemented.*

(EXPLANATION.)

This paragraph and those referred to in it, namely 306 and 311, especially the latter, require the following ends to be definitely secured:

1. Drawing the necessary line of distinction.
2. The provision of means for joint deliberation on matters of common interest to British India and the States, so as to ensure the

formulation of equitable decisions for India as a whole.

4. *That in order to define and secure the Political, Economic, Fiscal, and Financial interests of the States, a special Committee shall be appointed without delay, consisting of some such personnel as follows:*

(*a*) An eminent Jurist.

(*b*) A member of the Secretary-of-State's Council.

(*c*) A Political Officer.

(*d*) An Economist and Financier of European repute.

(*e*) A Financier from British India.

N.B. All these must be selected with an eye to their inspiring confidence in the minds of the Indian States.

(*f*) Some Ruling Princes.

(*g*) Some Ministers of States.

This Committee, it is recommended, should be presided over by a distinguished statesman of the type of Lord Robert Cecil, or Lord Ronaldshay.

5. *That the terms of reference of the Committee should be framed upon the following lines:*

(*a*) Assuming that an element of responsibility will be introduced in the Government of

India under a future instalment of Constitutional Reforms; or the powers now exercised by the Secretary-of-State for India will be transferred to the Governor-General-in-Council, what would be the relations of the Indian States to:

(1) His Majesty's Government,

(2) The Government of India?

Whether there would be any, and, if so, what, changes in the relation of Indian States to the Governor-General-in-Council when the centre of responsibility is shifted from the Secretary-of-State to the Central authority in India?

(*b*) What would be the authority competent to legislate on questions jointly affecting British India and the Indian States? And if the concurrence of the Indian States is regarded as essential for such legislation, what measure would be necessary to secure such assent?

(*c*) If the Indian States are to have an effective voice in matters of common concern to the whole country, what measure in the way of joint deliberation or otherwise would be most effective to secure that end?

(*d*) What would be the machinery to rectify violations of Treaties and Engagements subsisting between the States and external authority?

(*e*) Where the interpretation of Treaties and Engagements is affected by reference to the body of political usage and practice, what method should be adopted for assimilating with the Treaties and Engagements such practice and usage as are acceptable to the States, finally eliminating all unacceptable accretions which are fundamentally opposed to the spirit of those Treaties and Engagements?

(*f*) If the Provincial Governments are to receive a larger measure of control over their own affairs, should not the autonomy of the States be correspondingly extended?

(*g*) The desirability of instituting an independent Supreme Court of Appeal to take cognizance of and decide matters in issue between States *inter se* and between any Indian State and the Government of India or any Provincial Government. Matters not privately adjusted between the parties shall be referred to this Court at the option of either party and its decisions shall be binding on both parties.

(*h*) What should be the constitution and functions of the future Political Department of the Government of India and of its officers accredited to the Courts of Indian States?

(*i*) To inquire into and report on any disabilities and hardships imposed upon the subjects of Indian States by the financial and fiscal policy of British India, and to recommend the method of the removal of those hardships and disabilities.

(*j*) To consider all burdens imposed on subjects of Indian States by the financial and fiscal policy of the British Indian Government, and to weigh the benefits received by such subjects in return, or denied to them, and to recommend measures which would restore the balance in equity and justice.

(*k*) To consider any other matters relating to the interest, dignity, and privileges of the States.

APPENDIX II

SPEECH DELIVERED BY THE CHANCELLOR TO THE BUTLER COMMITTEE (1928)

SIR HARCOURT BUTLER, Members of the Indian States Committee: The protracted inquiry which has occupied you so long is now approaching its concluding stages; but before it terminates I am anxious to take advantage of your indulgence in order to give expression to some of the feelings which I know well are common to me and to my brother Princes. I will not detain you very long.

I am quite sure that from the commencement of your labours, Mr. Chairman, you and your colleagues shared with the Princes an anxiety to obtain as much information as possible bearing upon the problems which stand to be investigated. We acknowledge the courtesy with which you have afforded us the opportunity of collecting evidence in our endeavours to put forward a comprehensive case. We further acknowledge the patience which you have displayed in arranging for these protracted Sessions. We hope that we have shown that on our side neither energy nor expense has been spared in our endeavours to provide you with all the assistance in our power. But there was one factor over which neither you nor we could exercise complete control; and that is the factor of time. You, Sir Harcourt, possess a profound knowledge of the essential elements of the problems which you and your colleagues are investigating; but I may perhaps venture to question whether at the commencement of this inquiry, you had formed an estimate, any more accurate than that which we ourselves had formed, as to the time really requisite for the preparation of our case. We Princes have done our best; our Counsel, our Special Organization and our Ministers have laboured devotedly. But the fact remains that the time at your disposal and at ours has been all too short to enable us to do even the barest justice to the case which we desire to put before you. This shortness of time has been responsible for certain defects, to which I would briefly draw your attention. In the first place, it has handicapped the Members of the Chamber. Had more time been available, there can be little doubt but that the States who have authorized us to speak for them would be even more numerous than they are to-day. By way of illustration, I may mention the fact that even since your Committee commenced its Sessions in London, four more States have joined us—Cooch Behar, Bhawalpur, Dewas Junior, and Tehri Garhwal; and I think that if there had been sufficient opportunity for me and my colleagues of the Standing Committee to explain more fully to our brother Princes the aims and objects of our activities, we should have been able to appear before you with the declaration that the Princes of India spoke with a unanimous voice. If this consequence of the shortage of time has operated to handicap us, there is a further consequence which, if I may say so, has operated to handicap the Committee also, and that is the visible marks of haste which are so apparent in the evidence which we have placed before you. I do not here refer merely to certain minor misprints and misplacements in the printed volumes. In my opinion, considering the short time at their disposal, the printers have worked something very like a miracle; and

I do not think that these small deficiencies are likely seriously to impede the work of the Committee. I refer to more serious considerations. In the first place, the quantity of the evidence which we have placed before you would have been very largely augmented, had it been possible to spend a larger amount of time in its collection. It may perhaps surprise the Committee to learn that almost one-fourth of the States who are associated with the Standing Committee have found themselves unable to submit evidence in the detailed form upon which our Counsel has rightly insisted. This, of course, does not mean that these twenty States have got no cases. In reality, they possess many important ones. But in the time at their disposal, some of the States whose archives are not systematically arranged, have found it impossible to search out all the documents necessary for the proper establishment of the contentions they desire to put forward. Not only has the quantity of the evidence thus been diminished by the shortage of time; but in some respects its quality has also been affected. Our Counsel has already explained to you that the selection of evidence presented to you is merely representative. The task of selection would, I think, have been greatly facilitated had all the States which have joined us been able to submit their cases in the form which Counsel required. For we should then have been able to select as illustrations under every head a variety of instances fully illustrative of all the hardships from which the States are now suffering. Under many of the heads this has been done, but it will not have escaped the notice of the Committee that certain of the illustrations are of a kind which may appear, on superficial examination, somewhat trivial. I and my brother Princes feel the utmost confidence that the particular nature of these cases will not cause the Committee to overlook the fact that they frequently represent small examples of the violation of great principles. But it would have been more satisfactory, both to the Committee and to ourselves, if examples of these violations could have been in every case important of themselves, instead of merely important from their implication. There is no doubt that we could have put forward under a variety of heads better and more striking examples, had we been in a position to devote a longer time to the task of collection. Finally, having collected the evidence in an imperfect manner, we were also compelled to deal with it in a fashion far more summary than its importance demanded. I have been interested to learn that if we had entrusted the preparation of the presentation of our evidence to one of the most prominent firms of London solicitors, they would have required nearly twelve months, and a special staff, in order to deal satisfactorily with these four volumes which have been put into your hands. Had time been available, we should not have dreamed of asking you to consider the evidence in this comparatively undigested form. Our Counsel would have been able to reduce the case to a series of general propositions, illustrated by particular examples. Thus the value of the evidence would have been easier to estimate; and its total effect would have been more obvious. I fear, therefore, that we have to convey to you, Sir Harcourt, and to your colleagues, our regretful apologies for the manner in which we have had, quite involuntarily, to add to your already burdensome labour. But I trust I have said enough for you to realize that we have done our best despite many handicaps. Not the least of these handicaps, to be entirely frank, is the long-cherished belief of the States that their rights were perfectly safe; and that in view of the frequent and authoritative declarations made by the highest personages regarding the sanctity of the Treaties, they could rest secure; only recently has it been borne in upon the States that if the Crown is to protect them in the enjoyment of their rights and their privileges, they must be in a position to bring to its notice, clearly and precisely, the exact content of these rights. The result has been that, in past years, the Indian States have never even contemplated that a time might come when it would be necessary, in the interests of the Crown as well as of themselves, that they should put forward a reasoned case as against some of the actions of the Government of India. Such a supposition did not enter into their calculations. Their archives have never been arranged in such fashion as to facilitate it. Hence, when the necessity arose, it found the States almost entirely unprepared.

May I explain very briefly why we felt the need for the appointment of the present Committee? Our relationship with the Paramount Power goes back for a century and a quarter; and for roughly half that period, so far as my knowledge goes, it was never forgotten that the relationship of the States with the Crown was diplomatic; and that the rights and obligations of both parties, being enshrined in solemn documents, were entitled to the utmost respect. Official correspondence was still carried on in the language of the Mogul Court, courtesies were exchanged strictly in accordance with tradition, and every respect was shown to the position of the Princes as parties in contractual relations with the British. Where it became necessary, in pursuit of either political or humanitarian considerations, to enlist the co-operation of the States in matters affecting their own internal affairs, the process employed was invariably diplomatic in form. The abolition of slavery, suttee, and infanticide was obtained in such fashion and no other.

But when the British became paramount over the whole of India, their representatives turned naturally to the development of that portion of the country for whose administration they were directly responsible. Their desire to do their best for the great charge communicated to them, naturally led them to set a high value upon the virtues of efficiency and the methods of standardization. They began to conceive far-reaching policies for the benefit of British India; and the application of these policies came in time to embrace even the territories for whose admission Britain was not responsible. But almost up to the last decade of the nineteenth century, though pressure was unquestionably exerted upon the States in order to obtain from them agreements whose object was the enhancement of British-Indian revenues, the arrangements in connexion with salt, opium, railways, and the like were still concluded, in the letter but not in the spirit, with the consent of the States. The almost irresistible process which was making towards economic and even political unity throughout India, regardless of the privileged position in which the States stood towards the Paramount Power, was reinforced by internal developments in British India. The spread of Western Education, which Britain to her credit has always encouraged, led to a demand for the admission of British Indians to the Councils of their Government. In larger and larger measures the British principle of associating the governed with the Government, has been applied; with the natural result that the interests of British India and of its people came to bulk more and more largely in the estimation of the Government of India. If we consider the length of the period which has elapsed since the Mutiny, and the powerful operation of these forces, economic and political, which I have briefly mentioned, we shall not be surprised at the development of a position in which the Indian States find themselves to-day. For our own part, we are convinced that this position accords ill either with the treaty rights of the States, or with those interests which the British power has from time to time pledged itself to respect. The economic interests of the States, and the prosperity of the States' peoples, have unquestionably suffered; and we hope that we have brought to the notice of the Committee sufficient evidence to show upon how solid a basis our contentions rest. I could, if necessary, quote the words of British Officials of the highest rank in further support of the States' contention that the present position is unsatisfactory and calls for redress and for amendment.

We ourselves have for long been only too clearly aware of this. We knew we were in the position of allies. We had no doubt that our treaty rights were being infringed in a variety of directions. But until we took the unprecedented step of obtaining the best legal advice available, as we are not lawyers, we were working to some extent in the dark. The legal position has now been fully cleared up, for the first time, I believe, since the Indian States came into relations with Britain. The names of the Counsel who have subscribed to the legal opinion we have placed in your hands, carry an authority which cannot be questioned. I am informed that in accordance with the great tradition of the English Bar the opinion is a wholly impartial one; that our leading counsel, like his distinguished colleagues, was only concerned in the opinion to elucidate the legal position, whether it made for us or against us. The result you know. What we now seek is an official and effective recognition of the true position, that consent is the basis of our relationship with the Crown. Once this has been admitted, we Princes are prepared to negotiate with His Majesty's Government as to the machinery which will be necessary to ensure the preservation of our own rights as well as to promote the progress and prosperity of India as a whole. You will find us ready to co-operate with you in every reasonable way. But we do ask you to recognize the essential basis of our rights.

There is, however, one observation upon which I should like to lay great emphasis. I want to dissipate the impression that the Princes are plaintiffs, in a case where the Government of India are defendants. This is not so. The position as I see it is that the Indian States are doing their best to assist the Crown to establish a position which shall be satisfactory to both parties. If I may venture to say so, we are all sitting together as colleagues; and our one aim is to see that the true spirit of the relationship between the Indian States and the Paramount Power is in the first place elucidated and in the second place respected. If we have placed before you instances which seem to us to argue disregard of the States' rights and interests, it is only because we who wear the shoe may be expected to judge more particularly as to where that shoe pinches. We are not treating you as a criminal court and arraigning the Government of India before you; we are only doing our best to place before you the manner in which, as it seems to us, the present political system fails to secure the due discharge of those mutual rights and obligations which together constitute the bond between the States and the Crown. We feel that, unless we elaborate before you both the variety and the extent of those encroachments upon the rights of the States which the existing system has made possible, you as a Committee would scarcely be in a position to judge as to the extent to which the system requires rectification.

I should like, if you will allow me, to speak with the utmost frankness and to express, as perhaps only an Indian Prince can, some of the ways in which I and my colleagues conceive that the present system does lasting injury to the relationship, of which we are so proud, between ourselves and the Crown. The first point to which I should like to draw the attention of you,

Sir Harcourt, and of your colleagues, is the peculiar position in which those servants of the Crown, whose function was originally that of diplomatic agents, now find themselves placed. The Political Officer accredited to the Court of an Indian State is invested with an artificial authority which can be used, and is occasionally used, in a fashion which must necessarily reduce for the subjects of that State the effectiveness of the Ruler and of his administration. The Political Officer has come to be regarded, not merely as a representative, for diplomatic purposes, of the Paramount power, but as constituting in himself the embodiment of paramountcy. The use which he makes of his position is, in general, a matter of the personal equation. The Indian Princes acknowledge, and gladly acknowledge, that in the person of the Political Officers accredited to them, they have on occasion found their best, their wisest, and their most sympathetic friends. But at the same time we cannot ignore the fact that the position in which the Political Officer is placed enables him at any time to interpose his authority between the Ruler of a State and that Ruler's subjects. Where such interposition takes place, the results are disastrous. If once it is recognized that the Political Officer is willing to receive and to countenance complaints against the Ruler and his administration, then immediately such an Officer becomes the refuge of all who are discontented and all who desire to evade the responsibilities which they owe to the State. The Ruler and his administration are regarded as under the orders of the Political Officer. Not only does their prestige suffer, but their sense of responsibility is gravely affected, and their power for good unduly lowered and diminished. There is another side to this question. If the authority of the Political Officer is interposed between that of the Ruler and the Ruler's subjects, there is an inevitable tendency for the Ruler to conclude that his security and his reputation depend more directly upon the goodwill of the Political Officer than upon the happiness and the contentment of the people of the State. Such a state of affairs is disastrous. According to the ideas of Indian kingship, Ruler and people must ever remain face to face; so that while the subjects do not evade their obligations to the Ruler, the Ruler is equally unable to escape the duties which he owes to his subjects. Where an alien authority in the shape of a Political Officer intrudes itself between Ruler and ruled, the sense of responsibility of the Rulers is naturally weakened; the obligations owed by the ruled are transferred to an alien power.

The Princes of India frankly recognize the right of the Crown under the treaty relationship to assert its authority for the correction of gross injustice or flagrant misrule. But we are clearly of the opinion that such an obligation does not confer a right upon the agents of the Government of India to interfere at their own discretion with the internal administrations of the States. We realize that the British Officer, when accredited to the Court of an Indian State, may be expected to display a zeal for the introduction of administrative methods to which his own training has accustomed him. We realize that he may be expected to believe that the standards of administration appropriate for British India are equally applicable to the Indian States, whatever may be their individual stages of development. But we most earnestly desire to suggest that these natural tendencies should be restrained by the consideration that Western institutions, Western standards, and Western customs, are not necessarily suitable to polities where Ruler and ruled who are of one race, and who thoroughly understand one another, are still closely bound together by the ties of traditional sentiment. In this respect, we frankly look for help to the Crown. We hope that it will bring to the notice of its Political Officers that the ancient customs and the long-standing traditions of the Indian States have an intrinsic value of their own, and a part to play even in the world of to-day; that they do not depend for their survival upon the half-contemptuous toleration of the British Government. We would also earnestly ask that same Government, in the interests of relations which exist between the Indian States and the Paramount Power, to discard some of those notions of prestige which have already wrought such grave harm. We Princes of India are only too ready to co-operate with the Government of British India in the pursuit of aims which will redound to the advantage of the country as a whole. We would only ask that our co-operation should be invited; that the reasons underlying Government policy should be explained to us; and that where action on our part is desired, we should be satisfied of the necessity of the measure in question. I would ask the Committee to believe that it is in no spirit of fault-finding that I say that the present conditions are far different from those which I had indicated. Too often, when we Princes have to transact business with the representatives of the Government of India, we feel we are meeting men who are rigidly bound by certain instructions from which they cannot depart. We feel that their minds are already made up; that the issues under discussion are prejudged, and that their one aim and object is to induce us by any possible manner of means to acquiesce in views which have already been formulated. I would respectfully maintain that in such circumstances as these justice and equity cannot flourish. If we are to co-operate wholeheartedly with the Government of India and with its Officers, we must do so in a spirit of give and take. The intercourse between us must be of a kind which exists between persons who desire to reach an equitable decision after frank and free discussion. We cannot be expected to open our hearts in the presence of Officials who treat their own opinions and their own judgements as the epitome of wisdom, and who regard honest differences from their point of view as partaking of the nature of personal affronts. We earnestly hope that as the result of the representations we are making before the Committee, the Paramount Power will not only admit, but will impress upon its representatives, the position which we regard as fundamental: namely, that the States have a perfect right, outside the limits of the paramountcy agreement, to decline propositions of which they do not approve; and that it is not correct for every servant of the Government of India to look upon himself as the representative of a power which has the right, as well as the physical force, to impose its will upon the States in every particular.

We Indian Princes feel that if we are to discharge our obligations to the Crown, we must be placed in a position in which we can do our duty. We feel that through the operation of the existing political system, we have lost initiative and sense of responsibility. Whatever may have been the ideas underlying that system, its practical effect has been to keep us in leading-strings. But we feel that unless we are allowed to buy our experience, no matter at what cost, unless we are brought face to face with the consequences of our own actions so far as our subjects are concerned, we can never fully rise to the responsibilities of the position in which we have been placed by Providence, in appealing to a Committee composed of Englishmen. I think it is hardly necessary for me to justify a desire which I know is shared by my brother Princes, that in the sphere of sovereignty which remains to us, however great or small that may be, we should in truth be masters. But such an aspiration is all too frequently misunderstood. When some of us stand firm upon our rights as we conceive them to be, when we attempt, as loyal friends and allies of the Crown, to establish firmly our authority within our States, we are forthwith accused of cherishing ridiculous aspirations towards complete independence, and of manifesting a spirit of hostility to Britain. No assurances of mine, I feel confident, are necessary to demonstrate to such a Committee as this, the irresponsible, the wholly untrue, character of these suggestions. But the mere fact that they can be made, and are made, in the case of those of us who take our responsibilities, both to the Paramount Power and to our own people, most seriously, is surely an indication that something is wrong. What that something is we look to the Committee to discover. But for our own part we believe that it arises primarily from the fact that no definite and separate machinery has ever been set up to preserve and safeguard the spirit of the relationship between the Indian States and the Crown. The Political Department, whose services to the States we all of us frankly recognize, is after all but one branch of the Government of India. And if the Government of India is committed by its position to take a predominantly British-Indian view, then the Political Department, as a part of that Government, has to act under the orders which it receives. If the Government of India, in the discharge of its responsibilities towards British India, concentrates its attention primarily upon the development of British-Indian resources, and upon schemes for the progress of British India, it is only natural that the rights of the States and of their subjects should fall into a secondary place.

Inevitably, in such conditions as these, the interests of the States are subordinated to those of British India; and the Political Department, despite the best efforts of many admirable officers, tends to become merely the instrument by which this subordination is enforced. I desire to make plain, once and for all, the attitude of myself and my colleagues towards the whole of this vital inquiry. We are profoundly loyal to the person of His Majesty the King-Emperor; we are equally loyal to the obligations imposed upon us by our Agreements with the Paramount Power. We admit the rights which that Power is entitled to claim under the Agreements; we look to it to see that our own rights are equally secure. We have not the slightest wish to go outside the Empire. We only desire that the true spirit of the relationship between ourselves and Britain shall be respected. We have nothing but the friendliest feelings towards that Department of the Government of India which is primarily concerned with the transaction of our day-to-day business; we desire only that it should be placed in a position in which it is free to respect, and to mould its conduct in accordance with, the treaty relations. Incidentally, we have no hostility towards British India, and we do not desire to oppose its aspirations. We recognize that the question of political advance in that part of the country is a matter for settlement between British India and Great Britain. But our basic attitude can be summarized in a single sentence. We want to maintain our link with Britain. We believe that our relations are, and have always been, with Britain, and it is to the spirit of these relations that we desire to remain as true in the future as we have done in the past. We hope that there is nothing unreasonable in this desire. We feel that we are appealing to a power which has manifested so great a regard for the sanctity of solemn pledges that it entered the greatest war in history in defence of its plighted honour. We believe, and firmly believe, that the ties of obligation existing between Great Britain and ourselves are no less sacred than those which exist between Great Britain and Belgium.

May I close upon a note of personal appeal? I would beg of you, Sir Harcourt, and members of the Indian States Committee, when you are drafting your Report, to remember the manner in which the Indian Princes stood firm by Britain in 1857 and in 1914. As we have stood by you in the past, so we will stand by you in the future. We are putting forward no claim, we are raising no contention which we do not regard as fully justified by agreements which your Sovereigns have declared to be sacred and sacrosanct. We trust to you to see that this great opportunity is not lost. We have exposed to you, as frankly as we were able, what we regard as being the defects of the existing system by which our relations with the Crown are conducted. We have demonstrated to you our difficulties; we have shown you something of our grievances. We believe that wisdom and policy will alike dictate that steps should be taken to confirm and strengthen our devotion to the King-Emperor and to the British connexion, by vindicating our claim to those privileges which have been guaranteed to us, and by securing to the people of our States that treatment to which they are in all equity entitled. Finally, I would beg of you to remember that at a time when a large section of politically minded British India was boycotting the Simon Commission, because the method laid down for the inquiry was not pleasing to it, we Princes have from the very beginning co-operated whole-heartedly with you. What the Simon Commission will recommend for British India I do not know. But I respectfully submit that it would be the part of statesmanship for Britain to consider carefully the respective claims of those who have chosen the path of boycott and of those who have co-operated. I trust it will never be said that the people of British India obtained justice from Britain by boycotting the Simon Commission, while the Princes, people and States of Indian India were penalized, were disappointed of their rights, and were sent empty away, when they had co-operated to the utmost of their capacity in the work of the Indian States Committee.

APPENDIX III

NOTE ON THE ALLOCATION OF SEATS

At the first Round Table Conference, and particularly in the meetings of the Federal Structure Committee, it was repeatedly made clear, on behalf of that section of the Indian States' Delegation which represented the overwhelming majority of the States participating in the Chamber of Princes, that

(1) less than 125 seats in the Upper House for the Indian States would create great difficulties in providing for the due and adequate representation of the various States, and particularly of the 109 States which, in their own right, are at present Members of the Chamber of Princes; and

(2) however intrinsically sound the scheme of Federation and the provisions relating thereto might otherwise be, the question of the adequate representation of the States and the allocation of seats *inter se* would be one of the most important factors which would, in itself, determine the decision of the Princes whether to federate or not.

2. These important considerations have since also been reiterated in the Chamber of Princes, and on other occasions, on behalf of the States as a body, as well as by some important Rulers individually; and they were also stressed at the third Round Table Conference by Sir Manubhai Mehta and Nawab Sir Liaqat Hyat Khan, who were among the representatives of the Chamber of Princes and the Princes' Standing Committee. It had, however, been made clear all along that should any generally accepted scheme be evolved, by the British Government or any one else, the Princes would doubtless be prepared to consider it, on its merits, in a constructive spirit with an open mind, provided that the rights and interests of the States, big and small, were properly safeguarded, and their due and adequate representation secured to them.

3. The original discussions at the Federal Structure Committee of the first Round Table Conference were on the assumption that the Upper House would be a very small body in which the States would probably have not more than 50 seats allotted to them, in any case much less than 80. In the proposals emanating from

the Second Round Table Conference the number of States' seats was raised to 80. In view of its having been pointed out all along that even 80 seats were wholly inadequate for the purpose of providing due and adequate representation for such a large number of States, big and small, it is at least gratifying to see that the States' quota has now been raised to 100 in the White Paper. But, as even the number of 100 seats is 25 less than what was consistently pressed for on behalf of the States generally as the minimum necessary for providing for the equitable and reasonable representation of all the interests concerned, some of the difficulties anticipated still remain, even though the increase from something like 50 to 100 seats for the States has certainly improved matters.

4. Unfortunately the increase of 20 seats has been more than absorbed by the proposal to give larger representation to Hyderabad, the remaining four 21 gun States, the 19 gun States, and a selected number of the 17 gun States.

5. It would therefore be idle to disguise the fact that these tentative proposals of His Majesty's Government have caused profound disappoint-

ment, anxiety, and alarm generally amongst the great majority of the 109 States which are members of the Chamber of Princes in their own right, including also some of the important States. And it would indeed be no exaggeration to state that, so far as the States as a whole are concerned, the very scheme of Federation is likely to be seriously jeopardized on account of the various classifications, differences, and invidious distinctions involved in the proposed allocation of seats which, it will be apparent, reflect on the izzat, dignity, and importance *inter se* of even the larger and important States.

6. The strength and the volume of the feeling amongst the great majority of the Sovereign States on a question like this, which so vitally affects their izzat and status, as well as their Sovereignty and interests, have not been fully appreciated. A feeling exists among many States that it seems to have been assumed that, with the adhesion of a few of the larger States, the remaining States, both important and small, would, willingly or unwillingly, have come into the Federation.

. . . . .

14. Nothing has created more bitterness and

resentment amongst the Princes and States generally, than the attempts which have been made of late to belittle the importance of other States by suggestions that the Indian States are, or should be, grouped or graded into various classes or categories, which would derogate from their legitimate position and due importance and detract from their relative dignity and izzat, and automatically involve a stigma of inferiority of rank and status. Whilst, of course, there must, in the very nature of things, be, comparatively speaking, larger and smaller and more important and less important States, all having their relative seniority and juniority even amongst States in the same group of salutes, the only two well-known and accepted broad categories into which the Indian States have so far been divided for the purpose of comparison, without detracting in any way from their sovereign status, are the larger or more important States and the smaller States. These are the two classifications which have generally been applied to the Indian States, as, for instance, when the membership of the Chamber of Princes was under discussion just before its inauguration some 12 or 14 years ago.

Even in Europe, with a variety of States, the division ordinarily heard of is:

(1) the bigger States or Powers, and

(2) the small States.

A perusal of the proposed grouping of the States under six different categories will naturally be taken by the States generally as reviving the state of affairs which existed in Kathiawar, where the States were grouped under seven different classes, for the discontinuance of which invidious distinctions it is believed H.E. Lord Willingdon was personally responsible when he was Governor of Bombay.

. . . . .

17. Even though salutes serve to some extent as a useful guide in certain directions, it will be generally agreed, for reasons which will be obvious, that they cannot be taken as the sole or infallible test, since there are glaring anomalies in the existing table of salutes which have been publicly and officially admitted. Speaking on a somewhat similar question of the qualifying tests for membership of the Chamber of Princes, then about to be inaugurated, and when the constitution of that body was under discussion,

the Viceroy (Lord Chelmsford), in his speech at the Princes' Conference on the 20th January 1919, said that Mr. Montagu, the then Secretary-of-State for India, and he were of the opinion that

'the whole question of salutes needed most careful investigation in view of the anomalies which appear to exist, and they held, therefore, that it would be unwise to base upon the salute list, as it stood, any fundamental distinctions between the more important States and the remainder'.

Again, at the next Princes' Conference on the 3rd November 1919, the Viceroy referred to the same question in the following words:

'Your Highnesses will remember that in my last speech I said that Mr. Montagu and I felt that the whole question of salute needed most careful investigation in view of the anomalies which appeared to exist. If the principle which I now advocate is to be adopted as the basis of classification it will be additionally desirable that this investigation should be undertaken at an early date, in order that anomalies, whether already existing, or likely to ensue, from the institution of the dividing line, should be corrected wherever possible. My Government are ready to give their earnest consideration to this matter, and will make the necessary recommendations to the Secretary-of-State for submission to His Imperial Majesty in due course.'

18. Further, if the scheme of representation were to be based chiefly or exclusively on salutes, the question would also arise as to what would happen if, as is to be hoped, with a view to removing these admitted anomalies, or in the ordinary course otherwise, the salutes of any or a certain number of States were to be raised after the Federation and after the States' seats had been definitely allocated. As regards the Lower House, a provision is to be found in at least some Constitutions for the periodical revision, after each census, of the seats allotted to the States on the population basis. But since the States are represented in the Upper Chamber as sovereign States and Governments, it is scarcely conceivable that there will be a re-allocation of seats, some of which, then, would doubtless be at the expense of other States who may not have received an increase in salutes, for the benefit of those States whose salutes may hereafter be increased.

Viewed from all standpoints, and irrespective altogether of any personal considerations for the smaller or the larger States, it would appear that some more clearly defined principles and tests will have to be applied if plural representation is given effect to. From the very beginning the majority of the States in the Chamber have emphasized, on the basis of principles accepted in most federal constitutions, that there should be equality of representation for federal units as sovereign States and Governments in the Upper House. The question was one of principle; and a reasonable compromise on the basis of equity and justice had never been ruled out. If, however, for the purpose of determining the extent of representation, the rank and importance of States as indicated by permanent dynastic salutes and other important factors are to be taken into consideration, then the scheme which minimizes divergence of representation and, at the same time, provides each State with an effective voice in the Upper Chamber, is doubtless more likely to find acceptance among the vast majority of the States, than the one which gives, even to some of the senior 13 and 11 gun States, only alternative representation, say one such opportunity in 21 or about 28 years.

APPENDIX IV

SPEECH IN THE CHAMBER OF PRINCES

(January 1935)

THE Resolution which I now rise to move is, undoubtedly, the most important one on the agenda. It is the result of our discussions and deliberations in the Standing Committee and in the informal Conference of Princes, and I trust it will be carried unanimously. All that the Resolution purports to do is to reaffirm the willingness of the Princes and States of India to enter a Federation with British India under the aegis of the Crown, if the safeguards for their internal sovereignty and autonomy and other conditions are fully provided in the Constitution, and the scheme itself is acceptable to the other parties concerned. This has been our position from the beginning. This Chamber has, during the past four years in its annual sessions, reiterated that view without modification or variation.

While the position of the Princes remains therefore unchanged, the question whether the conditions which they laid down from the beginning have been satisfactorily met can only be decided after the Bill has been carefully scrutinized by experts. The Joint Parliamentary Committee's Report no doubt elaborates the scheme in many of its details, but until we are able to study the actual clauses of the Bill and the detailed provisions regarding many matters in which we are interested, it will, I hope, be appreciated that the Princes will not be able to decide definitely the question of their accession to Federation. But I may say here that, on a first examination, we are advised that some important questions like the financial conditions precedent to a federation, specially in regard to direct taxation, and the content of federal subjects, are left vague and undefined. In certain matters the powers of the Federation have been enlarged, as, for example, in the jurisdiction of the Federal Court. Subjects which had never been discussed with us have, in some cases, been added to the Federal list. On many points further elucidation seems to be necessary, as the recommendations of the Report seem ambiguous and capable of different interpretations. Besides, the Treaties of accessions, which will be the instruments binding the States, remain yet to be negotiated. It is essential that this supremely important document should be drawn up in consultation with the Princes and not as a unilateral agreement.

Resolutions of this Chamber during the last four years have again and again affirmed the desire of the Princes that a satisfactory determination of their rights and status should precede any invitation to the Princes to join a Federation. In view of the special powers vested in the Governor-General and Viceroy to protect the rights of the Princes, it seems essential that these rights should be authoritatively determined. In my speech at the first Round Table Conference I made this point unequivocally clear. It is true that this is a matter that the Joint Parliamentary Committee could not have discussed in their Report, but that does not make a negotiated settlement of this important question any the less imperative. With the inherent rights of the States remaining as undefined as they are to-day, it is difficult for the Princes to consider any scheme of political reform. That was, and remains, one of our essential conditions, as explained to the Government of India and His Majesty's Government We have not yet been informed what their views are on this matter; nor have we been invited to enter into further negotiations.

I desire also to emphasize one important point which I am glad to notice neither the Government of India nor His Majesty's advisers in England have overlooked. The Representatives of the Princes have, from the beginning, laid it down as a condition that, even if the Federal scheme is constitutionally unobjectionable, each State must have the absolute and unqualified freedom of choice to accede to, or to stand out of, the Federation. The choice must remain with each Ruler to decide whether his State should agree to join an All India Constitution. Let us not forget that the change that is suggested, whether beneficial or otherwise, is of a most momentous character. It would undoubtedly involve a fundamental change in our relations with British India. From politically separate entities in all matters, the States under a federation will become politically united with

British India in certain specified matters. Common institutions, common policies, common responsibilities will arise which in the Federal field will unite the States and British India into one whole. No one would deny that these are fundamental changes at which the most courageous and stout-hearted champions of the proposals may feel legitimate qualms, while others, to whom Federation was no more than an idea, will undoubtedly feel alarm and anxiety.

Nor can it be forgotten that Federation, in however modified a form, would involve vague and indefinite responsibilities for the future, from which the Princes, in their present position of isolated sovereignty, are practically immune. Even the Report of the Joint Parliamentary Committee does not conceal that fact. No constitution, however rigidly defined, can finally limit the liabilities of its constituent units in regard to defence and finance—the two most vital aspects of a Government. Who is there who would deny that in a federal constitution to which the States are parties, the constituent units, in future, will have to face liabilities and responsibilities which cannot now be estimated?

Nor are we entitled to forget that this Government of a united India, once established, will grow and continue to grow in a manner which we cannot foresee now. No institution devised by man develops exactly as its originator intends; least of all a constitution which vests great power and gives legal, executive, and judicial authority, no doubt in specified matters, over a whole country. Unforeseen conditions develop; circumstances not contemplated at the present time come into being, and the Federal Government may be forced, even if it were unwilling, to expand its function and even its scope. We have the example of the United States, and even of Imperial Germany, to show that even when a State's rights were rigorously and almost religiously safeguarded in the Constitution, the Central Governments have inevitably encroached on the powers of the constituent units.

Your Excellency, Your Highnesses. Do not think that I am arguing against a Federal Constitution. All that I desire to point out is the momentous character of the issue before the Princes. It is easy for people unconnected with the States to say 'Why do not the Princes declare their final intention?' It is easy for them to say that the Princes are vacillating, hesitant, and doubtful. If I may respectfully say so, the issue is not so simple as others imagine. We have a heavy and tremendous responsibility placed on us. We have to consider the sacred trust handed over to us by our ancestors; we have to think of the generations to come, and see that it is not said of us that we lightly signed away our States, prerogatives, and privileges which the courage, foresight, and wisdom of our forefathers had bequeathed to us. Equally, we have to take into consideration the conditions of the present day, and to safeguard ourselves against the wholly untrue accusation that we are less patriotic than our brethren in British India. We realize that the spirit of isolation can no longer be maintained; that institutions have to be devised for closer co-operation between the two Indias, that in matters of common concern it is in our interests to associate ourselves with British India. It is, therefore, no easy matter for us to come to a wise conclusion on a question so complicated, so fundamentally different from all other questions with which we had to deal as Rulers, so vitally affecting our States, ourselves, and our dynasties. May I, therefore, emphasize again that the discretion of each State in this matter remains totally unfettered?

The circumstances under which some of us agreed to consider a Federal proposal, as providing a suitable scheme of co-operation between British India and the States, are indeed well known. It was not from any desire on our part to hinder British India in the realization of its legitimate aspirations, but rather to help India in her constitutional progress and political development, without sacrificing our own sovereignty and internal autonomy; but to-day responsible men in British India, men who I know bear no ill will towards the States, have not hesitated to say frankly that in the present scheme of things, Indian States have become a positive hindrance rather than help to British India. I would not have taken such an expression of views, from however eminent a quarter, seriously but for the fact that it seems to be widely held in all sections of political opinion in British India. And if that is the view of men of moderation in the country, it is a matter for Your Highnesses seriously to consider whether we should put ourselves in the position in which practically every important body of opinion in British India considers us unwelcome partners, and looks upon our entry into Federation with suspicion. The benefits of a Federal scheme to the Indian States are, in any case, not so overwhelming that, whatever the opinion of British India, it would be in our interest to join in. On the other hand, if, as it would seem, the invitation of British India, which we willingly accepted, does not stand, and the benefits to the States are not obvious, the Princes for their part should be prepared to say, that while they are willing, as they have always been, to enter into a Federation, they would be equally prepared to stand out of a Federal scheme if British India is not anxious to have it. In view of the accusation that is being levelled against the States, I think it is necessary that our views should be clearly and unequivocally stated on this issue.

The changing attitude of British India towards the States—the accumulated evidence of which is known to all of you—has been of service to us.

In some ways it has been a source of enlightenment to us. It has enlightened us about the motives which animate even the most friendly among them to accept the idea of our association with them. They have made no secret of those motives. Those of the Indian politicians who desire our entry into the Federation, do so in the hope that in the near future we will be forced by circumstances to introduce in our States democratic forms of government. We are thankful that our friends in British India should have given us a clear indication of their views. While we can assure them that the Princes of India have always been willing to do whatever is best for their people, and will always be ready to accommodate themselves and their constitutions to the spirit of the time, we must frankly say that if British India is hoping to compel us to wear on our healthy body-politic the Nessus shirt of a discredited political theory, they are living in a world of unreality. It is well to clear all misconceptions. If the Princes decide to enter the Federation, they will do so with their eyes open, with the firm determination to cultivate feelings of friendship with British India, and co-operate with them in all matters concerning the welfare of this great country. But they will under no circumstances permit the utilization of the constitution for interference between themselves and their people. It must be clearly understood that the Princes will accept no constitution which would even by implication vest in any authority except themselves the right to decide their relations with their own people, the right to modify or alter their own polities, their right to live in the manner they and their people choose.

If, however, the critics of the States have in their mind the belief that they could assume political power in India, without taking into consideration the claims of the States and the just rights of the Princes, I would in all friendliness but with all firmness say that such a course would never be acceptable to the States. The sovereign rights, prerogatives, and privileges of the States are inherent in them and are guaranteed by solemn treaties. The Crown is under the most sacred obligation to keep them inviolate and inviolable, and there is no authority which can in any manner and at any time encroach upon them or question their validity. The idea that the States and their Rulers are an anachronism in the political life of India to-day, that they are merely apocryphal passages in the history of India, interpolated by a Machiavellian hand, which could be torn away without affecting the whole, is so utterly unhistorical as to require no comment. If British India desires to go forward without the association of the States, we shall have no complaint. The States of India stand by their own internal strength, by the loyalty of their people to their Rulers, by the bond of affection and attachment which unites the Princes and their people. They are rooted in age-long history, and I have the faith in me that, Federation or no Federation, the States of India will exist as integral parts in the polity of this great country, so long as the Rulers are true to their tradition of *Raj Dharma* and to their trust.

Your Highnesses, I confess I am an optimist. I have firm faith in the future of our States and of our Order. If British India is prepared for a Federal constitution, and that constitution assures us our rights of internal sovereignty, does not weaken the ties that bind us to our people and the Crown, secures to us our essential terms, and does not impose unbearable burdens on our finance, we shall, as we have always said, join it. But let me say it most emphatically, we are not enamoured of a Federal constitution as such; we have never approached H.M. Government and requested them to devise a Federal constitution in order to safeguard our future. If the Crown and British India, as the other parties to the constitutional development of India, desire the establishment of a Federal constitution, we for our part will be prepared to consider it sympathetically and with every desire not to stand in the way of the attainment by India of its status.

Do not let me be misunderstood. I have never hesitated to express my fervent desire that this great motherland of ours should occupy a most honoured place in the British Commonwealth of Nations, knowing full well that the greatness of India is also the greatness of her Princes. Patriotism is not the monopoly of any group, and the Indian Princes are no less patriotic than the rest of India's sons. Our desire that

India should advance along right lines has been expressed authoritatively on every suitable occasion. But the States have also their future to consider, and I shall not be a party, and I am sure none of Your Highnesses will be, to any scheme of advance which denies to the States of India their rights and authority. The history of India and the tradition that our ancestors have bequeathed us, entitle us to hope that if we face with courage and wisdom the issues before us, we shall triumph over this crisis as we have triumphed over others in the past. It is for that wisdom and courage that I pray, and I beseech Your Highnesses, whatever decision you take, to be true to your trust.